2004 SPECIAL!

G000161105

HARGREAV

MATCH Editor > Simon Caney **Art Director** > Darryl Tooth **Book Editor** > Ian Foster **Assistant Editor** > Kevin Hughes **Production Editor** > James Bandy
Deputy Production Editor > Kevin Pettman **Senior Writer** > Giles Milton **Sub-Editor/Writers** > Mark Bailey, Darren Cross **Senior Designer** > Martin Barry
Designer Calum Booth **Staff Photographer** > Phil Bagnall **Cartoonist** > Russ Carvell **And the rest of the MATCH team** > Dawn Brown, Isobel Cardew, Matt Read

First published 2004 by Boxtree an imprint of Pan Macmillan Ltd. Pan Macmillan, 20 New Wharf Road, London N1 9RR. Associated companies throughout the world. www.panmacmillan.com
ISBN 0752225472 Copyright © Emap Active Ltd 2004. The right of MATCH to be identified as the author of this work has been asserted by him in accordance with the Copyright, Designs and
Patents Act 1988. All rights reserved. No part of this publication may be reproduced, stored in a retrieval system or transmitted, in any form, or by any means (electronic, mechanical, photocopying,
recording or otherwise) without prior permission of the publisher. Any person who does any unauthorised act in relation to this publication may be liable to criminal prosecution and civil claims for
damages. 9 8 7 6 5 4 3 2 1 A CIP catalogue record for this book is available from the British Library. Colour Origination by Gildenburgh Reprographics. Design by MATCH. Printed by Proost, Belgium.

MATCH THE UK'S BEST-SELLING WEEKLY FOOTBALL MAGAZINE! MATCH
Bushfield House, Orton Centre, Peterborough, PE2 5UW ★ Tel: 01733 237111 Fax: 01733 288150 ★ e-mail: match.magazine@emap.com

DID YOU KNOW...?

CROATIA STRIKER DADO PRSO SCORED FOUR GOALS FOR MONACO WHEN THEY BEAT DEPORTIVO LA CORUNA 8-3 IN THE CHAMPIONS LEAGUE!

Come on England! Check out me wicked Euro 2004 scoutin' mission on page 95!

ENGLAND ON FILM!

Ashley Cole was caught sleeping on the job!

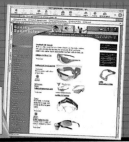
ATCH WAS THERE TO CATCH DAVID MES, ASHLEY COLE, KIERON DYER D JERMAINE JENAS RECENTLY HEN THEY WERE MODELLING SOME F UMBRO'S WICKED NEW ENGLAND LOTHING RANGE! WE RECKON THE DS LOOK WELL FLASH - BUT WE PE ENGLAND LOOK EVEN BETTER HEN THEY'RE WHUPPIN' FRANCE D ALL THE REST OF EUROPE'S NEST IN PORTUGAL THIS SUMMER!

YOU WANT ME TO MARK ASHLEY COLE? OKAY, NO PROBS!

YOU WHAT? HANG ON!

YOU WELL NEED A SHAVE, JAMO!

Jenas had to stop to read MATCH!

HEY SHORTY, BEHIND YOU!

EURO 2004 GIANTS!

Jan Koller
Czech Republic
6FT 8INS

Edwin van der Sar
Holland
6FT 6INS

Petr Cech
Czech Republic
6FT 4INS

Francesco Toldo
Italy
6FT 4INS

David James
England
6FT 3INS

10 WAYS TO STOP FRANCE'S THIERRY HENRY!

1 Tie his shoelaces together so he can't run properly!

2 Tell him that Euro 2004 has been switched from Portugal to Austria!

3 Lock him in a flashy Renault Clio and take away his Va Va Voom!

4 Pay Zinedine Zidane loads of cash not to pass to him!

5 Get Peter Reid to coach him for a few days – that'll make him rubbish!

6 Kidnap the France star and put him on a rocket into space!

7 Invent a time machine and send him back to 1,283 BC!

8 Buy a hungry crocodile and get it to eat the Arsenal ace!

9 Get Rik Waller to sit on him for the whole of June and July!

10 Sign him up to Big Brother and get him locked in the house!

TALENTLESS.

PAST IT.

HI BECKS!

HOW YOU DOING?

FIGO GREETS BECKS IN TYPICAL STYLE!

BECKHAM

TION BY CHECKING MATCH'S TIP-TOP TV GUIDE, WHICH STARTS ON PAGE 6! WICKED OR WHAT?

DID YOU KNOW...?

FRANCE 'STAR' DJIBRIL CISSE IS MISSING EURO 2004 AFTER HE WAS SENT OFF IN AN UNDER-21S MATCH. THE FIVE-MATCH SUSPENSION MEANT FRANCE COULDN'T CALL CISSE UP!

COUNTING THE COSTA!

Portugal ace Rui Costa is hiding in Planet Footy! But how many times can you find him? (Answer on p.63!)

THE COUNTRY

PORTUGAL

UEFA
Euro 2004
PORTUGAL

THE HOSTS → **PORTUGAL**

THE FINAL STADIUM

STADIUM OF LIGHT, LISBON

THE HOLDERS → **FRANCE**

THE OUTSIDERS

LATVIA

THE 30-SECOND GUIDE TO...
EURO 200[4]

THE MEGASTARS

THE POTENTIAL STARS

THIERRY HENRY

LUIS FIGO

DAVID BECKHAM

WAYNE ROONEY

JOAQU[IN]

THE DARK HORSES

CRISTIANO RONALDO

CZECH REPUBLIC

5 OVER-RATED EURO 2004 PLAYERS!

PATRICK KLUIVERT
HOLLAND

FREDI BOBIC
GERMANY

SYLVAIN WILTORD
FRANCE

DIEGO TRISTAN
SPAIN

ALEX DEL PIERO
ITALY

THE MASCOT

KINAS

KLOSE ENCOUNTERS

SO WHAT HAS GERMANY'S MIROSLAV KLOSE GOT UP CLOSE WITH NOW?

I LOVE GETTING UP KLOSE VITH STUFF, JA?

JA, I HAF JUST HAD A KLOSE ENCOUNTER WIF A GREAT VITE SHARK. IT VAS VERY SCARY!

OFFICIAL!

EVEN MY OWN MAMMA IS SCARED OF ME!

THE UGLIEST MAN AT EURO 2004!
Take a bow, Spain's Javi de Pedro!

DA EURO 2004 REFEREES

YOU MAY END UP SHOUTING AT THESE DUDES THIS SUMMER – BUT WHO THE HELL ARE THEY?

KIM MILTON NIELSEN – DENMARK

MIKE RILEY – ENGLAND

GILLES VEISSIÈRE – FRANCE

MARKUS MERK – GERMANY

PIERLUIGI COLLINA – ITALY

TERIE HAUGE – NORWAY

LUCÍLIO BATISTA – PORTUGAL

VALENTIN IVANOV – RUSSIA

LUBOS MICHEL – SLOVAKIA

MANUEL GONZÁLEZ – SPAIN

ANDERS FRISK – SWEDEN

URS MEIER – SWITZERLAND

WHO DA HELL IS EUSEBIO?

You might see some crumbly old Portuguese bloke called Eusebio popping up everywhere during Euro 2004! But who the flippin' heck is he? Pay yer respects to one of the world's best-ever players with our Five Fab Facts!

1 Eusebio is Portugal's greatest-ever footballer! He was a striker – a bit like Brazil legends Pele and Ronaldo – and was nicknamed 'The Black Pearl'!

2 He played in the great Benfica side of the 1960s, and won a massive 11 Portuguese Championships during his career!

3 He scored two goals in the final of the European Cup in 1962, as Benfica beat Real Madrid 5-3 in Amsterdam!

4 He was named European Footballer Of The Year in 1965 after Benfica reached their fourth European Cup final!

5 He starred in the 1966 World Cup as Portugal crashed out in the semi-finals to eventual winners England!

GIO'S EURO VERDICT!

Holland ace Giovanni van Bronckhorst reckons his side, along with France, are the faves to win Euro 2004! "Apart from us, I think it's got to be France, Germany, Italy or England," said the Arsenal man who's been on loan at Barcelona. "Portugal is in there with a shout as hosts, but if I had to choose I'd say the Netherlands or France!"

We reckon we can win the cup, for sure!

ENGLAND v FRANCE June 13

LISBON

ENGLAND v CROATIA June 21

So WHERE Do ENGLAND PLAY?
LISBON AND COIMBRA!

This summer, England will be playing their Euro 2004 group games in Lisbon and Coimbra. Can't get out there? Well let MATCH take you on a tour...

ENGLAND v SWITZERLAND June 17

COIMBRA

RED HOT SPAIN ARE READY!

Could this be the year Spain finally live up to their hype? They have the best league in the world but their national team has always disappointed in the major tournaments! This year, though, the word is that the Spanish side – led by Real Madrid star Raul – are set to challenge France, Italy, Portugal and England for the trophy!

This is how I'll pose for the team photo! Wicked!

Ivica Mornar — Croatia

Fabien Barthez — France

Jan Koller — Czech Rep.

Jaap Stam — Holland

Victor Onopko — Russia

Who said that?

That old guy in the cap looks stupid!

I kick ass every week for Real Madrid, and now I'll kick Euro 2004 ass!

Spain have got some top-class players!

England? Italy? France? Nah, Spain will win!

I'm better looking than Wayne Rooney any day!

FREDDIE LJUNGBERG'S EURO 2004 HAIR!

WHAT HAIRCUT WILL I BE WEARING AT EURO 2004?

MOHAWK

BUBBLE PERM

AFRO

SIDE-PARTING

PAVEL NEDVED'S euro dreamin'!

Czech Republic ace Pavel Nedved has been dreaming about getting his hands on the Euro 2004 trophy! The 2003 European Player Of The Year led his side to the finals in style and has set his sights on winning the competition! "To win Euro 2004 would be fantastic," said Nedved. "I have dreamt of picking up the trophy. We are not afraid of facing anyone!"

Dr. FOOTY SAYS: "Nedved is brilliant – all young players should learn from him!"

5 REASONS WHY THIS COULD BE SPAIN'S YEAR!

The Portuguese summer climate is very similar to Spain's, so the players will feel right at home!

The players are more motivated than ever to lift the trophy in Portugal, their local rivals!

Raul has disappointed in his last three major tournaments but now he's fully fit and raring to go!

Spain have a load of top young players like winger Joaquin and super striker Fernando Torres!

Their defence is even stronger since players like Barcelona's Carlos Puyol came into the side!

DON'T BE SO RUUD!

BARF!

Holland's cheeky striker Ruud van Nistelrooy is the king of bad manners, but how is he being rude now?

THIS TIME: PUKING IN THE EURO 2004 TROPHY!

DID YOU KNOW...?

ENGLAND WILL BE TRAINING AT THE OLD NATIONAL STADIUM IN LISBON DURING EURO 2004 – THAT'S WHERE CELTIC BEAT INTER MILAN TO WIN THE EUROPEAN CUP IN 1967!

HEAD-TO-HEAD

I'LL SCORE THE MOST GOALS IN GROUP A!

YEA... BUT I DO MO... STEPOV... SO EA... SOCK...

GOLDEN BOOT GAME!

1. CHRISTIAN VIERI
2. MICHAEL OWEN
3. RUUD VAN NISTELROOY
4. THIERRY HENRY
5. WAYNE ROONEY
6. RAUL

THE RULES!

1. Get five of your footy mates to play!
2. Write the numbers one to six on separate bits of paper, screw them up and stick them all in a hat!
3. Take it in turns to pull out a number – whoever picks No.1 gets striker No.1, whoever picks No.2 gets striker No.2 and so on!
4. The winner is the person whose striker nets the most goals at Euro 2004!

Behind-the-scenes at the...

ENGLAND TEAM HOTEL!

MATCH has found out where all the England players will be staying this summer – it's called the Solplay Hotel near Lisbon and it's so flash even J-Lo would love it there!

WHAT'S IN THE HOTEL?

★ A 35-seat cinema for movie-mad Kieron Dyer to watch his favourite flicks!

★ An on-site hairdresser so Becks can get a quick trim if he needs one!

★ Sound-proofed meeting rooms for Sven to explain all of his secret tactics!

★ A massive gym so David James can pump iron all day long!

★ An indoor and outdoor pool for swimming ace James Beattie to splash around in!

DID YOU KNOW? The hotel owner has offered to flatten the steps to the swimming pool so the England players don't trip up and injure themselves while they're there!

EURO HUNGRY?

What will the top footy stars be munching on before their big Euro 2004 matches?

ALESSANDRO DEL PIERO — SPAGHETTI BOLOGNESE!

IKER CASILLAS — PAELLA!

DAVID TREZEGUET — FROGS' LEGS!

MICHAEL BALLACK — SMELLY SAUSAGES!

THOMAS GRAVESEN — DANISH BACON!

MATCHY'S TO WATCH

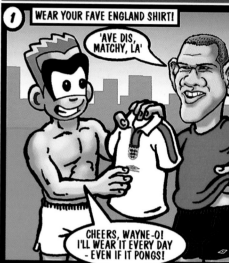

1 WEAR YOUR FAVE ENGLAND SHIRT!

'AVE DIS, MATCHY, LA'

CHEERS, WAYNE-O! I'LL WEAR IT EVERY DAY – EVEN IF IT PONGS!

4 CHECK OUT LATEST INF... MA...

WOWSERS! LITTLE MO'S TOP SCORER IN DA WHOLE TOURNAMENT! RESPEC'!

7 GO BANANAS WHEN BECKS SCORES AND ENGLAND WIN!

GOOOAAAL! INGER-LAND! INGER-LAND! INGER-LAND!

RYAN GIGGS WALES

ANDRIY SHEVCHENKO UKRAINE

ADRIAN MUTU ROMANIA

RUSTU RECBER TURKEY

DAMIEN DUFF REPUBLIC OF IRELAND

EURO 2004 GUIDE
NG INGER-LAND!

MATCH TRANSLATOR!

Whether you're off to Portugal this summer or just sat at home with your mates, try out these wicked Portuguese footy phrases!

There's only one Wayne Rooney!
Há somente um Wayne Rooney!

We're going to stuff France – eazee peazee!
Vamos bater a Franca – se problemas!

Quit diving Ronaldo, you cheat!
Para de mandares-te ao chao Ronaldo, batoteiro!

You only sing when you're winning!
Voces so cantam quand estao ganhando!

We're going to win the cup!
Vamos ganhar a taca!

England, England, England!
Inglaterra, Inglaterra, Inglaterra!

Don't touch the TV, mum!
Nao mudes o canal, mae!

Bring me some chips, I'm hungry!
Traga-me umas batatas fritas, estou com fome!

Who ate all the pies?
Quem comeu os empadoes todos?

Who the hell is Helder Postiga?
Quem e o Helder Postiga?

PUT AN ENGLAND FLAG IN YER WINDOW!

ANT RYBODZ TO OW I IS SUPPORTIN' GLAND! C'MON BOYZ!

3 GET SOMEBODY TO PAINT YOUR FACE!

CHEERS, RON! OI! D'YER WANT ME TO PAINT YER TEETH TOO?

WISH THE ENGLAND PLAYERS LUCK!

OD LUCK, CKS! SMASH A STOMPIN' EE-KICK R ME!

WILL DO MATCHY, SEE YA LATER!

6 PICK YOUR BEST ENGLAND TEAM!

JAMES

NEVILLE — RIO — COLE

CAMPBELL

BECKS — DYER

ROONEY — GERRARD

MATCHY — OWEN

UM, WHO SHALL I PICK UP FRONT? ME!

RELIVE THE GOALS WIV YOUR MATES!

RONALDO 9

AN' BECKHAM SHOOTS! WOT A GOAL!

9 GET READY FOR THE NEXT GAME!

COMING UP EURO 2004 ACTION

PHEW! I IS WELL TIRED! BUT DER'S EVEN MORE FOOTY ON DA WAY! GET IN!

THE TROPHY ROOM!
WHO'S BAGGED THE MOST EUROPEAN CHAMPIONSHIP TROPHIES?

GERMANY	3
FRANCE	2
DENMARK	1
HOLLAND	1
CZECH REP.	1
ITALY	1
SPAIN	1
RUSSIA	1

THU. JUNE 17 >> ENGLAND v SWITZERLAND ITV 5PM >> CROATIA v FRANCE BBC 7.45PM

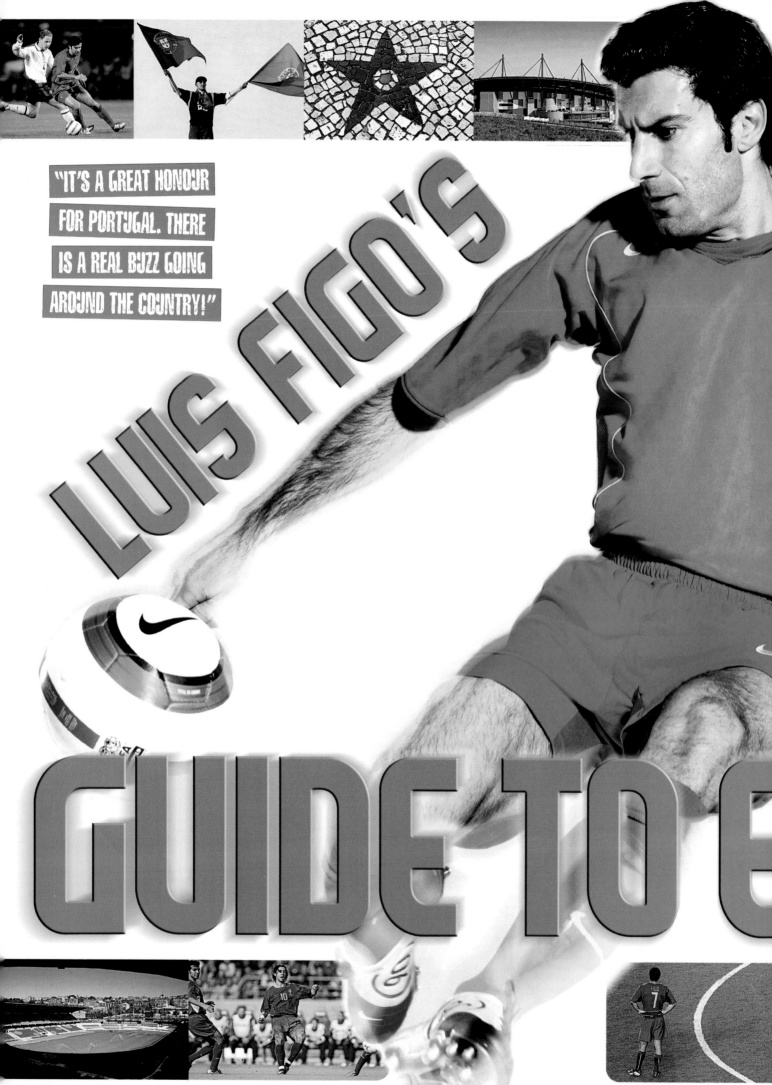

LUIS FIGO'S GUIDE TO E

LUIS FIGO, *the midfield magician of* **PORTUGAL**, *tells* **MATCH** *how the Euro 2004 hosts are preparing for Europe's biggest footy tournament!*

⭐ ARE YOU GETTING EXCITED ABOUT EURO 2004 NOW, LUIS?

"Definitely! It's a great honour for the whole of Portugal! It's a big thing for our people and there is a real buzz going around the country. We are very excited to have the top teams coming here and hopefully it will be a great tournament!"

⭐ DO YOU THINK PORTUGAL CAN GO ALL THE WAY TO THE FINAL?

"I don't know! That's impossible to answer. I think it depends a great deal on what sort of start we make in the group stages. But more importantly, we have to stay together and play as a team."

⭐ YOU'VE GOT AN EXPERIENCED COACH FOR THIS TOURNAMENT, HAVEN'T YOU?

"Yes, it is excellent to have a World Cup-winning manager in Luis Scolari. He gives the players the winning mentality that he has learned with the Brazil national team and the experience he has gained from the World Cup in Japan & South Korea. I think this can be a great advantage for us at Euro 2004."

⭐ WILL THERE BE A LOT OF PRESSURE ON PORTUGAL?

"In some ways there is always a lot of pressure, because we're playing at home and that carries a certain responsibility. But it could work in our favour if the fans can support us through the tough times and help us overcome any difficulties. We will be fine, because the crowd will be our 12th player. If this happens it will be a great advantage for us, but also a great responsibility."

⭐ WHAT CAN YOU TELL US ABOUT THE CURRENT PORTUGAL SQUAD?

"There have been major changes to the Portugal team which took part in Euro 2000 and the 2002 World Cup. You will see some players who have been in the Portugal side in previous tournaments, but they've been blended with youngsters who will be a big part of Portugal's future – so it should be very interesting!"

⭐ SO WE'RE GOING TO SEE A NEW GENERATION OF PORTUGAL STARS!

"Yes, I think it is natural that new talent will appear, because talented newcomers will always be given a chance if they have good individual skill. We have the likes of Rui Costa and Pauleta with lots of experience, plus players with great potential like Hugo Viana and Cristiano Ronaldo."

⭐ DO YOU THINK THIS IS THE BEST PORTUGAL TEAM EVER?

"I don't know, because I never had the chance to see the excellent Portugal team of 1966 that reached the World Cup semi-finals over in England! Unfortunately, I wasn't born then! But I think the quality of

URO 2004!

Portuguese players has been similar between that generation and those that have followed."

⭐ **BUT SURELY THE PLAYERS OF TODAY ARE BETTER THAN THE OLD ONES!**
"Ha, ha! No, I think the players from 1966 were similar to those of today's national team in terms of technical skill, because the Portuguese way of playing hasn't changed that much through the generations – whether it's the 1966 side, the 1980 side or our current team. I can't say more than that, because I wasn't around in 1966 so I never got the chance to see them!"

⭐ **FAIR ENOUGH! WILL YOU BE TURNING ON THE TRICKS FOR THIS TOURNAMENT?**
"Yes of course! There will be times where you try to produce some magic on the pitch – like a great dribble, a fantastic turn or scoring a brilliant goal!

Porto's Deco is a well tricky customer!

Portugal fans are colourful – and crazy!

Figo says Portugal are going all-out for glory at Euro 2004!

"WE ALL LOVE TO TRY OUT NEW TRICKS IN TRAINING, AND I GET TO MAKE A FOOL OF MY TEAM-MATES!"

These are all moments that the fans enjoy at the big tournaments, aren't they? They're the reason why people come to watch football in the first place."

⭐ **DEAD RIGHT! DO YOU SPEND TRAINING SESSIONS TRYING OUT NEW TRICKS?**
"Absolutely! We all love to try out new tricks in training and I get to make a fool of my team-mates! But I mean that in the best possible way – while still giving them the maximum respect, of course!"

⭐ **WILL THIS BE THE YEAR THAT PORTUGAL WIN THE EUROPEAN CHAMPIONSHIPS?**
"I certainly hope so! We will need some luck, because in this kind of competition luck can be very important! We might not have the same level of experience as some of the other teams in the finals, but we do have the Portuguese public on our side, which I hope will be an advantage and not a burden to our chances!"

The statue of Portugal legend Eusebio outside the Stadium Of Light in Lisbon.

Portugal have top young stars like Crissy Ronaldo!

A ROUGH GUIDE TO PORTUGAL!

Capital >	Lisbon
Flag >	
Population >	9,810,000
National dish >	Dried cod
Fave music >	Nelly Furtado, Maria Rita, Eminem
Fave other sport >	Golf

EURO 2004 STADIUMS

BRAGA MUNICIPAL
BRAGA
CAPACITY: 30,000

D. AFONSO HENRIQUES
GUIMARÃES
CAPACITY: 30,000

DRAGÃO STADIUM
PORTO
CAPACITY: 52,000

North Atlantic Ocean

Viana do Castelo

• Braga

Bragança

Vila Real

• Porto

AVEIRO MUNICIPAL
AVEIRO
CAPACITY: 30,000

Aveiro

• Viseu

• Guarda

SPAIN

Coimbra •

COIMBRA
COIMBRA CITY
CAPACITY: 30,000

DR. MAGALHÃES PESSOA
LEIRIA
CAPACITY: 30,000

Castelo Branco

Leiria •

BESSA STADIUM
PORTO
CAPACITY: 30,000

Santarem •

Portalegre •

Lisboa

Setubal •

• Evora

JOSÉ ALVALADE STADIUM
LISBON
CAPACITY: 52,000

LUZ STADIUM
LISBON
CAPACITY: 65,000

• Beja

Faro •

Gulf of Cadiz

ALGARVE STADIUM
FARO-LOULÉ
CAPACITY: 30,000

FIVE FAB PORTUGAL FACTS!

Portugal were once one of the world's great powers, and they had colonies all around the world in South America, Asia and Africa. In many South American countries like Brazil, they still speak Portuguese!

In Roman times, Portugal was called 'Luisitania'. The capital city Lisbon is still known as the 'City Of The Seven Hills'. That's because, unsurprisingly, it's very hilly in Lisbon!

The three biggest teams in Portugal are Benfica, Sporting Lisbon and Porto. Benfica won the European Cup in 1961 and 1962, while Porto lifted the trophy in 1987!

Sir Bobby Robson has managed Porto and Sporting Lisbon, while Sven Goran Eriksson has had two spells in charge of Benfica!

Portugal is ultra-popular with holiday-makers and averages around 27 million tourists a year! That's three times the amount of people who already live there!

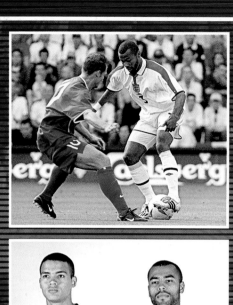

ENGLAND

SINCE 1872

F.C.

THE ENGLAND SQUAD!

Ace **ARSENAL** defender **ASHLEY COLE** introduces the **ENGLAND** superstars who'll be mixing it up in Portugal, as Sven's men go for Euro 2004 glory!

» DAVID BECKHAM «

Position: Midfielder ★ **Age:** 29

Club: Real Madrid

England caps/goals: 66/13

ASHLEY SAYS: "David is a great captain. He doesn't shout at you, he encourages you. Off the pitch he is always there for you – and that's what you need from a captain. He played with world-class players at Man. United, but at Real Madrid he's playing with the likes of Figo, Zidane, Ronaldo and Raul! And he can tell us about some of the French players as well!"

» WAYNE BRIDGE «

Position: Defender ★ **Age:** 23

Club: Chelsea

England caps/goals: 16/0

ASHLEY SAYS: "Wayne and I are good friends – we may be competing to play in the same position, but whatever happens we'll be friends. I support England and I want us to do well, but I don't want to give up the position and I'll try hard to keep it! When me and Wayne played together for England, I thought we did okay. But I'd rather play at left-back, so I could overlap him or swap positions!"

» NICKY BUTT «

Position: Midfielder ★ **Age:** 29

Club: Man. United

England caps/goals: 32/0

ASHLEY SAYS: "Nicky is really important to the England team – we need him to sit in front of the back four and command the defence, and he does a great job there. A lot of people said if you're not playing for your club, you can't play for England – but Nicky has already proved at the World Cup and in the Euro 2004 qualifiers that he's good enough to play for England."

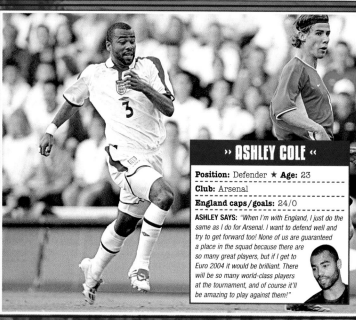

» ASHLEY COLE «

Position: Defender ★ **Age:** 23

Club: Arsenal

England caps/goals: 24/0

ASHLEY SAYS: "When I'm with England, I just do the same as I do for Arsenal. I want to defend well and try to get forward too! None of us are guaranteed a place in the squad because there are so many great players, but if I get to Euro 2004 it would be brilliant. There will be so many world-class players at the tournament, and of course it'll be amazing to play against them!"

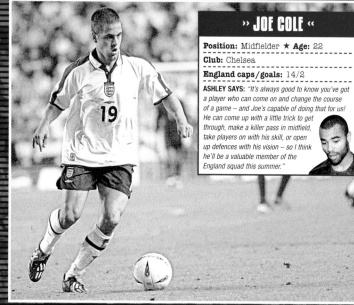

» JOE COLE «

Position: Midfielder ★ **Age:** 22

Club: Chelsea

England caps/goals: 14/2

ASHLEY SAYS: "It's always good to know you've got a player who can come on and change the course of a game – and Joe's capable of doing that for us! He can come up with a little trick to get through, make a killer pass in midfield, take players on with his skill, or open up defences with his vision – so I think he'll be a valuable member of the England squad this summer."

» KIERON DYER «

Position: Midfielder ★ **Age:** 25

Club: Newcastle

England caps/goals: 20/0

ASHLEY SAYS: "I think Kieron is a massive threat with his pace, and if he can get one-on-one with a defender he'll do some real damage! It's always nice to have quick players in the team because they can take players on, and Kieron is really direct. As soon as he gets the ball, you know he can get to the byline and cross it – and that'll be a great asset for our strikers."

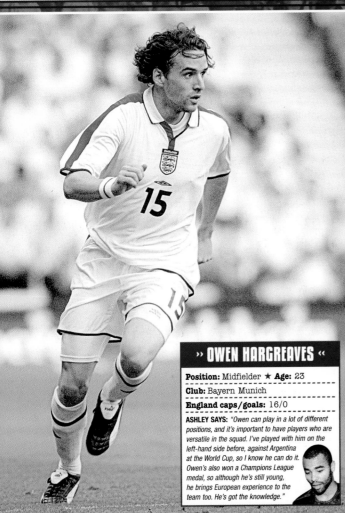

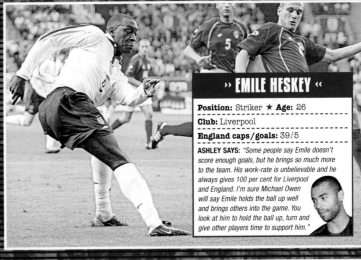

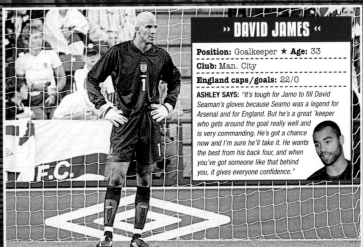

» FRANK LAMPARD «

Position: Midfielder ★ **Age:** 25

Club: Chelsea

England caps/goals: 17/1

ASHLEY SAYS: "Frank has had a great season for Chelsea, and for me he's definitely been one of the best players in the Premiership. He's been scoring a lot of goals from midfield, and I think he can bring that flair to the England team and maybe nick us a goal! Form is important, and if you're playing well for your club, then hopefully you can carry it on to the international stage."

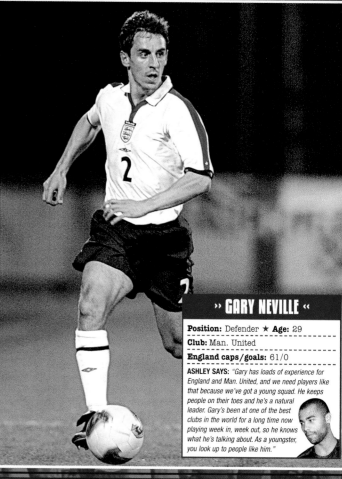

» GARY NEVILLE «

Position: Defender ★ **Age:** 29

Club: Man. United

England caps/goals: 61/0

ASHLEY SAYS: "Gary has loads of experience for England and Man. United, and we need players like that because we've got a young squad. He keeps people on their toes and he's a natural leader. Gary's been at one of the best clubs in the world for a long time now playing week in, week out, so he knows what he's talking about. As a youngster, you look up to people like him."

» MICHAEL OWEN «

Position: Striker ★ **Age:** 24

Club: Liverpool

England caps/goals: 54/24

ASHLEY SAYS: "Michael is a world-class striker. He has achieved so much in the game and he's already earned over 50 caps – even though he's about the same age as me, so it's a fantastic achievement for him! He's so quick and sharp, and you know with Michael that if you give him a chance, he'll put it away. You've got to have a player like that in your side at international level."

» WAYNE ROONEY «

Position: Striker ★ **Age:** 18

Club: Everton

England caps/goals: 10/3

ASHLEY SAYS: *"Wayne has been brilliant for England and when he's on the pitch, it just gives everyone else a buzz because we know what he can do! If you give him a chance he'll score – he's got a few goals for England already and he'll be getting service from players like David Beckham and Frank Lampard. I've had to mark him a few times in training, so I know he's a top player!"*

» JOHN TERRY «

Position: Defender ★ **Age:** 23

Club: Chelsea

England caps/goals: 6/0

ASHLEY SAYS: *"Rio's absence has left a hole in the defence and John Terry is more than capable of filling it. Rio's a great player and it'll be hard to fill his position, but John's a top player at a big club and he'll enjoy it. Rio and John are pretty similar in the way they command games, but they're different too. John is a die-hard defender, but both are great players in their own right."*

» PAUL SCHOLES «

Position: Midfielder ★ **Age:** 29

Club: Man. United

England caps/goals: 60/13

ASHLEY SAYS: *"I've spoken to some of the Arsenal players who say Paul Scholes is one of the best midfielders in the world – and to play with him is unbelievable! He hasn't scored for England for a few games, but he brings more to the side than just goals. His vision is amazing, he works well with David Beckham and Nicky Butt, and he adds so much to our team."*

EURO 2004

Your Ultimate Guide to the European Championships starts here, as **MATCH** reveals

KICK-OFF!

everything you need to know about the 16 teams who are chasing glory in Portugal!

GROUP A
PORTUGAL
GREECE
SPAIN
RUSSIA

PORTUGAL

Cristiano Ronaldo's got more tricks than an ace magician!

Portugal will be going all-out for Euro 2004 glory on home soil!

★ THE SQUAD ★

Goalkeepers

Quim
Club: Braga
Age: 28 ★ Caps/Goals: 19/0

Ricardo
Club: Sporting Lisbon
Age: 28 ★ Caps/Goals: 24/0

Quim.

Defenders

Paulo Ferreira
Club: Porto
Age: 25 ★ Caps/Goals: 9/0

Rui Jorge
Club: Sporting Lisbon
Age: 31 ★ Caps/Goals: 40/1

Fernando Meira
Club: Stuttgart
Age: 26 ★ Caps/Goals: 16/0

Miguel Monteiro
Club: Benfica
Age: 24 ★ Caps/Goals: 9/1

Jorge Andrade
Club: Deportivo La Coruna
Age: 26 ★ Caps/Goals: 18/2

Nuno Valente
Club: Porto
Age: 29 ★ Caps/Goals: 8/0

Beto
Club: Sporting Lisbon
Age: 28 ★ Caps/Goals: 28/2

Ricardo Carvalho
Club: Porto
Age: 26 ★ Caps/Goals: 2/0

Fernando Couto
Club: Lazio
Age: 34 ★ Caps/Goals: 103/7

Fernando Couto.

Rui Jorge.

Midfielders

Sergio Conceicao
Club: Porto
Age: 29 ★ Caps/Goals: 56/12

Rui Costa
Club: AC Milan
Age: 32 ★ Caps/Goals: 86/23

Costinha
Club: Porto
Age: 29 ★ Caps/Goals: 21/2

Deco
Club: Porto
Age: 26 ★ Caps/Goals: 10/1

Luis Figo
Club: Real Madrid
Age: 31 ★ Caps/Goals: 100/30

Ribeiro Maniche
Club: Porto
Age: 26 ★ Caps/Goals: 6/0

Petit
Club: Benfica
Age: 27 ★ Caps/Goals: 17/0

Cristiano Ronaldo
Club: Man. United
Age: 19 ★ Caps/Goals: 3/0

Tiago
Club: Porto
Age: 23 ★ Caps/Goals: 6/0

Hugo Viana
Club: Newcastle
Age: 21 ★ Caps/Goals: 11/0

Petit.

Strikers

Pauleta
Club: Paris St Germain
Age: 31 ★ Caps/Goals: 54/28

Helder Postiga
Club: Tottenham
Age: 21 ★ Caps/Goals: 2/2

Simao
Club: Benfica
Age: 24 ★ Caps/Goals: 24/4

Nuno Gomes.

Hugo Almeida
Club: Uniao Leiria
Age: 20 ★ Caps/Goals: 1/0

Luis Boa Morte
Club: Fulham
Age: 26 ★ Caps/Goals: 13/1

Nuno Gomes
Club: Benfica
Age: 27 ★ Caps/Goals: 36/14

Luis Boa Morte.

Can Euro 2004 hosts PORTUGAL win the trophy in front of the home supporters?

HOW DID THEY QUALIFY?

Er, they didn't have to! As hosts, Portugal qualified automatically for the competition, so while other teams have been busting a gut to make the finals, Portugal have been playing friendlies ever since they bombed out of the 2002 World Cup! They've played plenty of games during that time, but it'll be interesting to see if a lack of competitive action affects them.

WHAT ARE PORTUGAL'S STRENGTHS?

Portugal's number one advantage is that Euro 2004 is in their own back yard! Being the hosts they'll be used to the conditions, the stadiums – oh, and they'll have the whole country cheering them on too! That aside, they've got some ace players – from the old school of Figo, Rui Costa and Pauleta to young stars like Viana, Ferreira and Ronaldo.

AND THEIR WEAKNESSES?

While their blend of youth and experience could be seen as a good thing, it might prove to be Portugal's downfall. Some of the oldies look past it now, while some of the youngsters aren't ready to make the step up. More worrying, though, is that Portugal rely so heavily on Pauleta to score goals. Playing up front on his own, the PSG ace doesn't get much support, and if he's injured or off form, goals could be a problem.

HOW WILL THEY DO?

As the Euro 2004 hosts, Portugal will be gutted if they don't make it to the quarter-finals. With the quality they've got in the squad, that shouldn't be too much of a problem – but after an unconvincing display in the friendly against England, it'll be interesting to see if they can improve on their semi-final place at Euro 2000.

★ PORTUGAL'S STRONGEST LINE-UP ★

RICARDO

FERREIRA — COUTO — ANDRADE — RUI JORGE

COSTINHA — PETIT

FIGO — RUI COSTA — DECO

PAULETA

Sergio Conceicao's a real class act.

PORTUGAL STATS & FACTS!

MANAGER: Luis Felipe Scolari	**WORLD RANKING:** 17th
CAPTAIN: Fernando Couto	**ODDS TO WIN EURO 2004:** 13/2
MOST CAPS (Current Squad):	**PREVIOUS TOURNAMENTS**
Fernando Couto, 103	**EURO 2000:** Semi-finals
MOST GOALS (Qualifying):	**BEST EVER:** Semi-finals, 1984
N/A	& 2000

★ WHO PLAYED IN PORTUGAL'S FRIENDLIES? ★

PARAGUAY	BOLIVIA	KAZAKHSTAN	SPAIN	NORWAY	ALBANIA	GREECE	KUWAIT	ENGLAND
Drew 0-0 (h)	*Won 4-0 (h)*	*Won 1-0 (h)*	*Lost 3-0 (h)*	*Won 1-0 (a)*	*Won 5-3 (h)*	*Drew 1-1 (h)*	*Won 8-0 (h)*	*Drew 1-1 (h)*
Ricardo	Ricardo	Ricardo	Ricardo	Ricardo	Ricardo	Quim	Quim	Ricardo
Ferreira	Ferreira	Monteiro	M Ribeiro	Monteiro	Ferreira	Monteiro	Monteiro	Ferreira
Rui Jorge	Rui Jorge	Rui Jorge	Valente	Rui Jorge	Rui Jorge	Rui Jorge	Rui Jorge	Rui Jorge
Meira	Andrade 1	Meira	Meira	Andrade	Andrade	Andrade	Andrade	Andrade
Couto	Couto 1	Couto	Couto	Couto	Couto	Couto	Couto	Couto
Figo	Maniche	Figo	Figo	Figo	Figo 1	Figo	Figo 1	Figo
Maniche	Tiago	Costinha	Costinha	Costinha	Costinha	Costinha	Costinha	Costinha
Loureiro	Conceicao	Deco	Conceicao	Frechauf	Ronaldo	Deco	Deco	Petit
Rui Costa	Viana	Rui Costa	Rui Costa	Rui Costa	Rui Costa 1	Rui Costa	Rui Costa	Rui Costa
Pauleta	Postiga 2	Viana	Maniche	Boa Morte	Tiago	Boa Morte	Simao	Simao
Conceicao	Pauleta	Pauleta	Pauleta	Pauleta 1	Pauleta 1	Pauleta 1	Pauleta 4	Pauleta 1
Substitutes:	*Substitutes:*	*Substitutes:*	*Substitutes:*	*Substitutes:*	*Substitutes:*	*Substitutes:*	*Substitutes:*	*Substitutes:*
Deco 46	Six substitutes	Seven substitutes	Six substitutes	Beto Severo 65	Ten substitutes	Four substitutes	Five substitutes	Ten substitutes
Postiga 61		Simao 1 46		Deco 70	Simao 1 46		Gomes 3 66	
Silas 76					M Ribeiro 1 61			

★ PORTUGAL'S STAR MEN ★

LUIS FIGO ★ Midfielder

Portugal's talisman and 100-cap hero pulls the strings in midfield for the hosts, and he'll be desperate to take his team a step further than Euro 2000, when they made the semis. At 31, Figo is coming to the end of a brilliant international career, and he won't get many more chances of glory with his country.

RUI COSTA ★ Midfielder

The AC Milan midfielder is another veteran in Portugal's squad who'll probably be playing in his last major tournament. But even at 32, the playmaker can tear the opposition apart with a jinking run or defence-splitting pass. If Rui Costa can find some consistency, he'll be a force to be reckoned with at the finals.

PAULETA ★ Striker

Averaging a goal in every other game for Portugal, Pauleta could rip it up at the finals this summer! With his nifty footwork and movement, the PSG striker is sure to worry even the best defenders, and if he's given a sight of goal he'll make teams pay! Pauleta often plays up front on his own, but as long as he gets the support, he'll be a big threat.

MATCHMAN'S VERDICT!

"**Dem Portu-geezers is gonna be tough to beat in their own back yard but I don't recks they is da best team in da comp, so it's da semis for them!**"

GROUP A

PORTUGAL
GREECE
SPAIN
RUSSIA

GREECE

★ THE QUALIFYING SQUAD ★

Goalkeepers

Konstantinos Chalkias
Club: Panathinaikos
Age: 30 ★ Caps/Goals: 4/0

Theofanis Katergiannakis
Club: Olympiakos
Age: 30 ★ Caps/Goals: 6/0

Antonios Nikopolidis
Club: Panathinaikos
Age: 32 ★ Caps/Goals: 39/0

Antonios Nikopolidis.

Defenders

Traianos Dellas.

Panagiotis Fyssas
Club: Panathinaikos
Age: 31 ★ Caps/Goals: 27/4

Giannis Goumas
Club: Panathinaikos
Age: 29 ★ Caps/Goals: 25/0

Mihalis Kapsis
Club: AEK Athens
Age: 30 ★ Caps/Goals: 6/0

Sotirios Kyrgiakos
Club: Panathinaikos
Age: 24 ★ Caps/Goals: 9/1

Paraskevas Antzas
Club: Olympiakos
Age: 27 ★ Caps/Goals: 12/0

Christos Patsatzoglou
Club: Olympiakos
Age: 25 ★ Caps/Goals: 16/0

Nikos Dabizas
Club: Leicester
Age: 30 ★ Caps/Goals: 65/0

Giourkas Seitaridis
Club: Panathinaikos
Age: 23 ★ Caps/Goals: 15/0

Traianos Dellas
Club: Roma
Age: 28 ★ Caps/Goals: 13/0

Stylianos Venetidis
Club: Olympiakos
Age: 27 ★ Caps/Goals: 35/0

Midfielders

Angelos Basinas
Club: Panathinaikos
Age: 28 ★ Caps/Goals: 39/2

Giorgios Georgiadis
Club: Olympiakos
Age: 32 ★ Caps/Goals: 55/11

Stylianos Giannakopoulos
Club: Bolton Wanderers
Age: 29 ★ Caps/Goals: 34/7

Pantelis Kafes
Club: Olympiakos
Age: 25 ★ Caps/Goals: 17/2

Giorgios Karagounis
Club: Inter Milan
Age: 27 ★ Caps/Goals: 28/2

Pantelis Kafes.

Konstantinos Katsouranis
Club: AEK Athens
Age: 24 ★ Caps/Goals: 3/0

Pantelis Konstantinidis
Club: Panathinaikos
Age: 28 ★ Caps/Goals: 20/1

Vassilios Lakis
Club: AEK Athens
Age: 27 ★ Caps/Goals: 26/3

Vassilios Tsiartas
Club: AEK Athens
Age: 31 ★ Caps/Goals: 55/10

Theo Zagorakis
Club: AEK Athens
Age: 32 ★ Caps/Goals: 85/0

Theo Zagorakis.

Strikers

Ioannis Amanatidis
Club: Stuttgart
Age: 22 ★ Caps/Goals: 3/0

Angelos Charisteas
Club: Werder Bremen
Age: 24 ★ Caps/Goals: 24/7

Lampros Choutos
Club: Olympiakos
Age: 24 ★ Caps/Goals: 10/3

Themistoklis Nikolaidis
Club: Atletico Madrid
Age: 30 ★ Caps/Goals: 47/17

Dimitris Papadopoulos
Club: Panathinaikos
Age: 23 ★ Caps/Goals: 3/1

Zisis Vryzas
Club: Perugia
Age: 30 ★ Caps/Goals: 43/6

Ioannis Amanatidis.

It's smiles all round as Greece seal their place at Euro 2004!

They're outsiders to qualify from Group A, but GREECE will fancy their chances of an upset!

HOW DID THEY QUALIFY?

Greece caused a massive upset in qualifying by finishing top of their group – ahead of Spain and an Andriy Shevchenko-inspired Ukraine team! Better still, they did it after losing their first two games – against Spain and the Ukraine! But after that, they got maximum points – with the highlight being a 1-0 win in Spain, which meant Raul and co. finished runners-up in the group and had to go through the play-offs!

WHAT ARE GREECE'S STRENGTHS?

Greece have built their success on a solid defence, and the fact that they only conceded four goals in eight games against the likes of Raul, Reyes and Shevchenko says it all. They're a well-organised, hard-working unit, and although there are no superstars in the squad, everyone does their job.

AND THEIR WEAKNESSES?

Greece's defence is very good, but the team have struggled to score goals themselves. Despite winning Group 6, they only scored eight times in eight games, with Werder Bremen striker Angelos Charisteas top-scoring with just three. It's also the first time Greece have reached the European Championships for 24 years, so a lack of experience in major tournaments could count against them at Euro 2004.

HOW WILL THEY DO?

Host team Portugal and the exciting Spanish are the class sides in this group, and they're the favourites to progress through to the quarter-finals. But you'd be stupid to write off Greece – after all, they beat Spain to top spot in qualifying! Their lack of goals and big-game experience might count against them, but they've shown they can compete with some of the best sides in Europe – so if they can find the net regularly, then who knows?

★ GREECE'S STRONGEST LINE-UP ★

NIKOPOLIDIS

SEITARIDIS — DABIZAS — DELLAS — VENETIDIS

LAKIS — ZAGORAKIS — TSIARTAS — GIANNAKOPOULOS

NIKOLAIDIS — CHARISTEAS

The Greeks will build their campaign on a strong defence.

★ FINAL QUALIFYING TABLE ★

TEAM	P	W	D	L	F	A	PTS
1. GREECE	8	6	0	2	8	4	18
2. SPAIN	8	5	2	1	16	4	17
3. UKRAINE	8	2	4	2	11	10	10
4. ARMENIA	8	2	1	5	7	16	7
5. N. IRELAND	8	0	3	5	0	8	3

Greece were surprise winners of Group 6.

GREECE STATS & FACTS!

MANAGER: Otto Rehhagel

CAPTAIN: Theo Zagorakis

MOST CAPS (Current Squad):
Theo Zagorakis, 85

MOST GOALS (Qualifying):
Angelos Charisteas, 3

WORLD RANKING: 30th

ODDS TO WIN EURO 2004: 66/1

PREVIOUS TOURNAMENTS

EURO 2000: Did Not Qualify

BEST EVER: Quarter-finals, 1980

★ GREECE'S STAR MEN ★

GIOURKAS SEITARIDIS ★ Defender

Seitaridis has only been a professional for three years but in that time he's made a big impression. The 23-year-old is strong in the tackle, uses the ball well and loves to get forward – and these qualities have alerted some of Europe's top clubs, including Spain giants Valencia. One of Greece's top stars, he's definitely one to watch at Euro 2004!

VASSILIOS TSIARTAS ★ Midfielder

At 31, and with over 50 caps to his name, Vassilios Tsiartas brings a lot of experience – and a touch of flair – to the Greece midfield. The AEK Athens star, who has also played in Spain with Seville, likes to get on the ball and make things happen, with his set-pieces and long-range shooting a speciality.

ANGELOS CHARISTEAS ★ Striker

Greece's top scorer in qualifying, Charisteas will be hoping to take that kind of form into the finals. The 24-year-old striker enjoyed a great season with the Bundesliga's surprise outfit Werder Bremen, where the powerful striker's class and ability in the air shone through. Could be a big star at Euro 2004!

★ WHO PLAYED IN GREECE'S EURO 2004 QUALIFYING GAMES? ★

SPAIN	UKRAINE	ARMENIA	N. IRELAND	SPAIN	UKRAINE	ARMENIA	N. IRELAND
Lost 2-0 (h)	*Lost 2-0 (a)*	*Won 2-0 (h)*	*Won 2-0 (a)*	*Won 1-0 (a)*	*Won 1-0 (h)*	*Won 1-0 (a)*	*Won 1-0 (h)*
Nikopolidis	Nikopolidis	Nikopolidis	Nikopolidis	Nikopolidis	Nikopolidis	Nikopolidis	Nikopolidis
Patsatzoglou	Seitaridis	Seitaridis	Giannakopoulos	Seitaridis	Seitaridis	Seitaridis	Seitaridis
Fyssas	Venetidis	Venetidis	Venetidis	Venetidis	Fyssas	Fyssas	Fyssas
Dellas	Dellas	Dellas	Kyrgiakos	Dellas	Dellas	Dellas	Dellas
Dabizas	Dabizas	Dabizas	Dabizas	Dabizas	Dabizas	Antzas	Dabizas
Konstantinidis	Lakis	Basinas	Konstantinidis	Kapsis	Kapsis	Basinas	Basinas
Zagorakis	Zagorakis	Georgiadis	Zagorakis	Zagorakis	Zagorakis	Kapsis	Antzas
Tsiartas	Tsiartas	Kafes	Karagounis	Tsiartas	Lakis	Karagounis	Tsiartas 1
Giannakopoulos	Karagounis	Tsiartas	Tsiartas	Giannakopoulos 1	Karagounis	Giannakopoulos	Giannakopoulos
Charisteas	Charisteas	Charisteas	Charisteas 2	Tsiartas	Giannakopoulos	Charisteas	Charisteas
Nikolaidis	Nikolaidis	Nikolaidis 2	Nikolaidis	Tsiartas	Vryzas	Tsiartas 1	Vryzas
Substitutes:	*Substitutes:*	*Substitutes:*	*Substitutes:*	*Substitutes:*	*Substitutes:*	*Substitutes:*	*Substitutes:*
Basinas 46	Vryzas 65	Zagorakis 46	Vryzas 40	Lakis 34	Haristeas 1 46	Georgiadis 67	Nikolaidis 46
Vryzas 72	Giannakopoulos 66	Giannakopoulos 46	Fyssas 71	Karagounis 36	Choutos 65	Zagorakis 84	Georgiadis 46
	Basinas 69	Vryzas 60	Kafes 74		Tsiartas 71		Zagorakis 89

Nikos Dabizas.

MATCHMAN'S VERDICT!

"Greece was wicked in qualifyin' and now they is in da same group as Spain again! Portugal an' Spain are da faves to go through, but Greece is gonna have summat to say about dat!"

GROUP A

PORTUGAL
GREECE
SPAIN
RUSSIA

SPAIN

Real Madrid's Guti is just one of Spain's classy midfielders.

Raul is a goal machine for Real Madrid and Spain!

★ THE QUALIFYING SQUAD ★

Goalkeepers

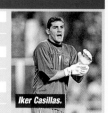

Iker Casillas.

Santiago Canizares
Club: Valencia
Age: 34 ★ Caps/Goals: 40/0

Iker Casillas
Club: Real Madrid
Age: 23 ★ Caps/Goals: 34/0

Pedro Contreras
Club: Real Betis
Age: 32 ★ Caps/Goals: 1/0

Defenders

Carlos Marchena.

Agustin Aranzabal
Club: Real Sociedad
Age: 31 ★ Caps/Goals: 28/0

Raul Bravo
Club: Real Madrid
Age: 23 ★ Caps/Goals: 9/0

Garcia Calvo
Club: Atletico Madrid
Age: 29 ★ Caps/Goals: 3/0

Ivan Helguera
Club: Real Madrid
Age: 29 ★ Caps/Goals: 39/3

Juanfran
Club: Celta Vigo
Age: 25 ★ Caps/Goals: 11/0

Juanito
Club: Real Betis
Age: 25 ★ Caps/Goals: 4/0

Carlos Marchena
Club: Valencia
Age: 24 ★ Caps/Goals: 13/0

Cesar Martin
Club: Deportivo La Coruna
Age: 27 ★ Caps/Goals: 9/2

Carlos Puyol
Club: Barcelona
Age: 26 ★ Caps/Goals: 24/1

Michel Salgado
Club: Real Madrid
Age: 28 ★ Caps/Goals: 33/0

Michel Salgado.

Midfielders

Gaizka Mendieta.

Jose Etxeberria
Club: Athletic Bilbao
Age: 26 ★ Caps/Goals: 48/12

Guti
Club: Real Madrid
Age: 27 ★ Caps/Goals: 10/2

Xavi Hernandez
Club: Barcelona
Age: 24 ★ Caps/Goals: 17/0

Gaizka Mendieta
Club: Middlesbrough
Age: 30 ★ Caps/Goals: 40/8

David Albelda
Club: Valencia
Age: 26 ★ Caps/Goals: 13/0

Xabi Alonso
Club: Real Sociedad
Age: 22 ★ Caps/Goals: 6/0

Ruben Baraja
Club: Valencia
Age: 28 ★ Caps/Goals: 29/6

Vicente Rodriguez
Club: Valencia
Age: 22 ★ Caps/Goals: 21/1

Joaquin Sanchez
Club: Real Betis
Age: 22 ★ Caps/Goals: 18/2

Juan Carlos Valeron
Club: Deportivo La Coruna
Age: 28 ★ Caps/Goals: 38/3

Strikers

Diego Tristan.

Raul Gonzalez
Club: Real Madrid
Age: 26 ★ Caps/Goals: 69/37

Alberto Luque
Club: Deportivo La Coruna
Age: 26 ★ Caps/Goals: 4/0

Fernando Morientes
Club: Real Madrid
Age: 28 ★ Caps/Goals: 30/20

Jose Antonio Reyes
Club: Arsenal
Age: 20 ★ Caps/Goals: 4/2

Fernando Torres
Club: Atletico Madrid
Age: 20 ★ Caps/Goals: 3/0

Diego Tristan
Club: Deportivo La Coruna
Age: 28 ★ Caps/Goals: 15/4

They've definitely got the players, but have SPAIN got the nerve to shine at Euro 2004?

HOW DID THEY QUALIFY?

Considering the easy group they were in, Spain made hard work of qualifying. After a good start, they drew 2-2 with the Ukraine, then lost at home to Greece and failed to break down a Northern Ireland side that finished bottom of the group. It meant Spain had to go into the play-offs, but they came good when it mattered. A 2-1 win over Norway at home was followed by a 3-0 whupping away!

WHAT ARE SPAIN'S STRENGTHS?

One of Spain's main strengths is they'll know exactly what to expect from the competition – they've been at every major tournament since Euro '92. They've also got some amazing young talent to go with the established world-class stars like Raul, Puyol and Helguera. If the likes of Torres, Reyes and Joaquin can shine, then Spain could go a long way.

AND THEIR WEAKNESSES?

They always bottle it on the big stage! Spain may have qualified for every tournament since 1992, but they've flopped at all of them! With the talent in their squad, they've often been tipped as dark horses for the World Cup and European Championships but then failed to deliver. Coach Inaki Saez and the Spanish public will be hoping it's different this time around, but they won't be holding their breath!

HOW WILL THEY DO?

Spain will hopefully learn a lesson after Greece beat them to the top spot in qualifying. They've been drawn in the same group again at Euro 2004, but it'll be a big shock if the Spanish finish lower than the Greeks again! With their sensational attacking quality, Spain should make the quarter-finals – but they'll need to hold their nerve when the pressure is on.

★ SPAIN'S STRONGEST LINE-UP ★

CASILLAS

SALGADO HELGUERA MARCHENA PUYOL

ETXEBERRIA BARAJA ALBELDA VICENTE

VALERON

RAUL

★ FINAL QUALIFYING TABLE ★

TEAM	P	W	D	L	F	A	PTS
1. GREECE	8	6	0	2	8	4	18
2. SPAIN	8	5	2	1	16	4	17
3. UKRAINE	8	2	4	2	11	10	10
4. ARMENIA	8	2	1	5	7	16	7
5. N. IRELAND	8	0	3	5	0	8	3

Juan Carlos Valeron keeps Norway at bay in the play-off.

SPAIN STATS & FACTS!

MANAGER: Inaki Saez	**WORLD RANKING:** 3rd
CAPTAIN: Raul	**ODDS TO WIN EURO 2004:** 7/1
MOST CAPS (Current Squad): Raul, 69	**PREVIOUS TOURNAMENTS**
MOST GOALS (Qualifying): Raul, 7	**EURO 2000:** Quarter-finals
	BEST EVER: Winners, 1964

CARLOS PUYOL ★ Defender

The Barcelona ace has emerged as one of Europe's top defenders, with Man. United one of his many admirers. It's not hard to see why either – Puyol can play anywhere across the back four, has lightning pace and loves to get stuck in. Opposition strikers had better beware when this fella's around!

JOSE ETXEBERRIA ★ Midfielder

With Raul often playing as a lone striker for Spain, it's left up to Athletic Bilbao winger Jose Etxeberria and Juan Carlos Valeron to bomb forward and help. Etxeberria has scored 12 goals from 48 games, and those goals – along with his pace and directness – make him a real star to watch in Portugal!

RAUL ★ Striker

The Prince of Spanish football will arrive at Euro 2004 in brilliant goalscoring form after hitting seven goals in ten qualifying games! The captain's ability to bring his team-mates into the game with his sublime skill is second to none and his finishing is deadly. The Real Madrid star is also Spain's top scorer ever with 37 goals – and he's only 26 years old!

MATCHMAN'S VERDICT!

"When is da Spanish gonna show wot they can do in a tournament? They've got da skills to pay da bills, but bottle it on da big stage. Quarter-finals but no more, I recks!"

★ WHO PLAYED IN SPAIN'S EURO 2004 QUALIFYING GAMES? ★

GREECE	N. IRELAND	UKRAINE	ARMENIA	GREECE	N. IRELAND	UKRAINE	ARMENIA	NORWAY	NORWAY
Won 2-0 (a)	Won 3-0 (h)	Drew 2-2 (a)	Won 3-0 (h)	Lost 1-0 (h)	Drew 0-0 (a)	Won 2-1 (h)	Won 4-0 (a)	Won 2-1 (h) *og	Won 3-0 (a)
Casillas	Casillas	Casillas	Casillas	Casillas	Casillas	Casillas	Casillas	Casillas	Casillas
Salgado	Salgado	Salgado	Salgado	Salgado	Puyol	Salgado	Salgado	Salgado	Salgado
Raul Bravo	Raul Bravo	Cesar	Raul Bravo	Raul Bravo	Juanfran	Puyol	Puyol	Puyol	Puyol
Garcia Calvo	Helguera	Aranzabal	Helguera 1	Puyol	Sergio	Juanito	Helguera	Helguera	Helguera
Marchena	Puyol	Marchena	Marchena	Marchena	Marchena	Marchena	Marchena	Marchena	Cesar
Joaquin	Joaquin	Etxeberria 1	Etxeberria	Etxeberria	Etxeberria	Etxeberria	Etxeberria	Etxeberria	Etxeberria 1
Helguera	Baraja 2	Baraja	Albelda	Helguera	Helguera	Baraja	Baraja	Baraja	Baraja
Valeron 1	Guti 1	Guti	Valeron	Valeron	Valeron	Xabi Alonso	Valeron 1	Albelda	Xabi Alonso
Xavi	Xavi	Albelda	Xavi	Vicente	Baraja	Vicente	Reyes	Valeron	Albelda
Vicente	Vicente	Vicente	Tristan 1	Morientes	Vicente	Fernando Torres	Vicente	Torres	Vicente 1
Raul 1	Raul	Raul 1	Raul	Raul	Raul	Raul 2	Raul 1	Raul 1	Raul 1
Substitutes:	*Substitutes:*	*Substitutes:*	*Substitutes:*	*Substitutes:*	*Substitutes:*	*Substitutes:*	*Substitutes:*	*Substitutes:*	*Substitutes:*
Mendieta 59	Morientes 63	Valeron 65	Joaquin 1 41	De Pedro 57	Morientes 65	Reyes 63	Reyes 2 62	Valeron 69	Guti 74
Baraja 59	Mendieta 76	Xavi 65	Vicente 53	Joaquin 57	Joaquin 65	Valeron 63	Xabi Alonso 66	Joaquin 78	Joaquin 78
Cesar 87	Capi 83	Tristan 77	Baraja 64	Sergio 76	De Pedro 79	Xavi 84	Luque 78	Vicente 78	Baraja 87

RUSSIA

★ THE QUALIFYING SQUAD ★

Goalkeepers

Igor Akinfeev
Club: CSKA Moscow
Age: 25 ★ Caps/Goals: 1/0

Viatcheslav Malafeev
Club: Zenit St Petersburg
Age: 25 ★ Caps/Goals: 1/0

Sergei Ovchinnikov
Club: Lokomotiv Moscow
Age: 33 ★ Caps/Goals: 29/0

Sergei Ovchinnikov.

Defenders

Dmitri Sennikov.

Denis Evsikov
Club: Lokomotiv Moscow
Age: 23 ★ Caps/Goals: 4/0

Sergei Ignashevitch
Club: CSKA Moscow
Age: 24 ★ Caps/Goals: 12/3

Yuri Kovtun
Club: Spartak Moscow
Age: 34 ★ Caps/Goals: 50/3

Gennadi Nizhegorodov
Club: Lokomotiv Moscow
Age: 27 ★ Caps/Goals: 9/0

Alexei Berezoutski
Club: CSKA Moscow
Age: 21 ★ Caps/Goals: 4/0

Vassili Berezoutski
Club: CSKA Moscow
Age: 21 ★ Caps/Goals: 2/0

Vadim Evseev
Club: Lokomotiv Moscow
Age: 28 ★ Caps/Goals: 6/1

Viktor Onopko
Club: Real Oviedo
Age: 34 ★ Caps/Goals: 110/7

Dmitri Sennikov
Club: Lokomotiv Moscow
Age: 27 ★ Caps/Goals: 11/0

Andrei Solomatin
Club: CSKA Moscow
Age: 28 ★ Caps/Goals: 13/1

Midfielders

Yevgeni Aldonin
Club: Rotor Volgograd
Age: 24 ★ Caps/Goals: 11/0

Dmitri Alenitchev
Club: Porto
Age: 31 ★ Caps/Goals: 49/6

Rolan Gusev
Club: Dynamo Kiev
Age: 26 ★ Caps/Goals: 23/1

Marat Izmailov
Club: Lokomotiv Moscow
Age: 21 ★ Caps/Goals: 15/0

Andrei Kariaka
Club: Krylia Sovetov
Age: 26 ★ Caps/Goals: 15/3

Marat Izmailov.

Dmitri Khokhlov
Club: Lokomotiv Moscow
Age: 28 ★ Caps/Goals: 46/5

Dmitri Loskov
Club: Lokomotiv Moscow
Age: 30 ★ Caps/Goals: 11/0

Alexandr Mostovoi
Club: Celta Vigo
Age: 35 ★ Caps/Goals: 63/13

Sergei Semak
Club: CSKA Moscow
Age: 28 ★ Caps/Goals: 38/4

Alexei Smertin
Club: Chelsea
Age: 29 ★ Caps/Goals: 37/0

Rolan Gusev.

Strikers

Vladimir Beschastnykh
Club: Spartak Moscow
Age: 30 ★ Caps/Goals: 71/26

Dmitri Bulykin
Club: Dynamo Moscow
Age: 24 ★ Caps/Goals: 5/4

Aleksandr Kerzhakov
Club: Zenit St Petersburg
Age: 21 ★ Caps/Goals: 15/3

Ruslan Pimenov
Club: Lokomotiv Moscow
Age: 22 ★ Caps/Goals: 4/0

Dmitri Sytchev
Club: Lokomotiv Moscow
Age: 20 ★ Caps/Goals: 13/3

Vladimir Beschastnykh.

Veteran Victor Onopko has won 110 caps for Russia.

Can RUSSIA surprise everyone and make an impact after qualifying through the play-offs?

HOW DID THEY QUALIFY?

Russia had to go through the lottery of the play-offs to book their place at the finals after finishing a point behind Switzerland in Group 10. They scraped past Wales 1-0 over two legs, but their place at the finals was thrown into doubt after Yegor Titov failed a drugs test after the first leg. Despite Welsh protests and Titov being banned, Russia have been allowed to take their place at Euro 2004.

WHAT ARE RUSSIA'S STRENGTHS?

If there's one thing you can say about Russia, they do score goals! They hit 19 of them in just eight qualifiers – and although they weren't playing against the best teams in Europe, it was still impressive. And the goals were spread around the side – with Dmitri Bulykin hitting four, defender Sergei Ignashevitch chipping in with three and the midfielders doing their bit as well!

AND THEIR WEAKNESSES?

Apart from blowing hot and cold, Russia's main problem in qualifying was how rubbish they looked on their travels – which doesn't sound too good for Euro 2004 in Portugal. They won all four games in their own back yard, but only managed two points on their travels – losing to Georgia and Albania! Another worry is the 12 goals they let in during qualifying – more than any other country who will play in this year's tournament!

HOW WILL THEY DO?

Looking at Group A on paper, you would have to tip Russia to struggle. Portugal and Spain are the best teams, while Greece are an organised, hard-working side who beat Spain to top spot in their qualifying group! That leaves Russia, who only just made the finals through the play-offs, are rubbish on their travels and leak too many goals. It doesn't look good – but that's the beauty of tournament footy!

★ RUSSIA'S STRONGEST LINE-UP ★

OVCHINNIKOV

EVSEEV IGNASHEVITCH ONOPKO SENNIKOV

SMERTIN SEMAK GUSEV ALENITCHEV

MOSTOVOI

BULYKIN

★ FINAL QUALIFYING TABLE ★

TEAM	P	W	D	L	F	A	PTS
1. SWITZERLAND	8	4	3	1	15	11	15
2. RUSSIA	8	4	2	2	19	12	14
3. REP. OF IRELAND	8	3	2	3	10	11	11
4. ALBANIA	8	2	2	4	11	15	8
5. GEORGIA	8	2	1	5	8	14	7

Russia celebrate after beating Wales 1-0.

RUSSIA STATS & FACTS!

MANAGER: Georgi Yartsev

CAPTAIN: Alexei Smertin

MOST CAPS (Current Squad): Victor Onopko, 110

MOST GOALS (Qualifying): Dmitri Bulykin, 4

WORLD RANKING: 24th

ODDS TO WIN EURO 2004: 66/1

PREVIOUS TOURNAMENTS

EURO 2000: Did Not Qualify

BEST EVER: Winners, 1960

★ RUSSIA'S STAR MEN ★

ALEXANDR MOSTOVOI ★ Midfielder

The 35-year-old Celta Vigo star might be coming to the end of his international career, but he'll want to bow out in style! Mostovoi is a tricky dribbler and pulls the strings either in midfield or just behind the lone striker – supplying him with plenty of ammunition. He scores goals too, so watch out for him!

ALEXEI SMERTIN ★ Midfielder

The Russia captain spent this season in the Premiership – on loan at Portsmouth after signing for Chelsea. For his country, Smertin does a good job of keeping things moving in midfield. He likes to get his foot in, but also keeps possession well with neat passing, which is important at international level.

DMITRI BULYKIN ★ Striker

Despite only making his Russia debut less than a year ago, Dmitri Bulykin has exploded on to the international scene. The powerful striker, who was linked with a January transfer window move to Everton, was his country's top scorer in qualifying with four goals from five games. If he can keep up that form at the finals, Russia could cause a shock!

MATCHMAN'S VERDICT!

"Dem Russians did well to beat Wales in da play-offs, an' they 'ave some class playerz an' all, but I can't see 'em gettin' outta da group stages. Cheerio dudes!"

★ WHO PLAYED IN RUSSIA'S EURO 2004 QUALIFYING GAMES? ★

REP. OF IRELAND	ALBANIA	ALBANIA	GEORGIA	SWITZERLAND	REP. OF IRELAND	SWITZERLAND	GEORGIA	WALES	WALES
Won 4-2 (h) *og	Won 4-1 (h)	Lost 3-1 (a)	Lost 1-0 (a)	Drew 2-2 (a)	Drew 1-1 (a)	Won 4-1 (h)	Won 3-1 (h)	Drew 0-0 (h)	Won 1-0 (a)
Ovchinnikov	Ovchinnikov	Ovchinnikov	Mandrikin	Ovchinnikov	Ovchinnikov	Ovchinnikov	Ovchinnikov	Ovchinnikov	Malafeev
Yanovski	Yanovski	A Berezoutski	Nizhegorodov	Yanovski	Evseev	Radimov	Evseev	Evseev	Evseev 1
Nizhegorodov	Nizhegorodov	Nizhegorodov	Semak	V Berezoutski	Sennikov	Solomatin	Sennikov	Sennikov	Sennikov
Ignashevitch	Ignashevitch	Ignashevitch	Ignashevitch	Ignashevitch 2	Ignashevitch 1	Ignashevitch	Ignashevitch	Ignashevitch	Ignashevitch
Onopko	Onopko 1	Tochilin	Onopko	Kovtun	Onopko	Onopko	Onopko	Onopko	Onopko
Semak	Semak 2	Semak	Aldonin	Semak	Mostovoi	Mostovoi 1	Mostovoi	Mostovoi	Izmailov
Aldonin	Smertin	Smertin	Smertin	Smertin	Smertin	Smertin	Kariaka	Smertin	Smertin
Gusev	Gusev	Gusev	Kariaka	Gusev	Gusev	Gusev	Gusev	Loskov	Gusev
Loskov	Solomatin	Aldonin	Izmailov	Aldonin	Essipov	Kariaka	Titov 1	Alenitchev	Alenitchev
Kariaka 1	Loskov	Loskov	Alenitchev	Popov	Alenitchev	Kerzhakov	Bulykin 1	Bulykin	Titov
Beschastnykh 1	Kerzhakov 1	Kerzhakov	Titov	Kariaka	Bulykin	Bulykin 3	Kerzhakov	Sytchev	Bulykin
Substitutes:	Substitutes:	Substitutes:	Substitutes:	Substitutes:	Substitutes:	Substitutes:	Substitutes:	Substitutes:	Substitutes:
Solomatin 29	Aldonin 46	Solomatin 50	Evsikov 15	Sytchev 46	Kerzhakov 34	Sennikov 46	Izmailov 45	Izmailov 46	Radimov 59
Kerzhakov 1 46	Yevseyev 78	Kariaka 1 55	Kerzhakov 46	Bistrov 51	Aldonin 39	Izmailov 55	Sytchev 1 56	Gusev 59	
Khokhlov 75	Popov 63	Yanovsky 73	Sytchev 80	Evsikov 81		Sytchev 76	Aldonin 63		

How to celebrate... Like Italy!

ONE PERSON...

...THEN MORE...

...THEN BUNDLE

STEALING, WITH JORG STIEL!

Another day, another crime, with Switzerland's light-fingered 'keeper!

Yeah, I just pinched Tower Bridge from London! Don't reckon nobody will notice, y'nah-worram-sayin'?

FIGO wants to go out on top!

FIGO 7

Wicked Portugal midfielder Luis Figo is planning his perfect international retirement gift – the Euro 2004 trophy! Figo will quit international footy after this summer's tournament and wants to go out on a massive high by leading his side to victory on home soil! "Playing in front of the Portugal fans in my home country is the best way to end my international career," the Real Madrid star revealed. "But winning a major trophy would be even better!"

MATCHY SAYS: "Nice one! Figo 'as gotta be one of da biggest stars in da game! Footy will well miss 'im!"

WHAT LOVELY THICK HAIR YOU HAVE!

THANKS!

DO! Flatter the gaffer!

THE DO'S AND DON'TS OF...

EURO 2004 EN

OH HOKEY-COKEY!

STRIKE COMIN' UP!

DO! Make sure you're wearing the right boots!

DO! Join in all the silly dances!

OI LADS, WHICH ONES ARE MINE?

GIRLY EURO 2004 NAMES!

KIM KALLSTROM
SWEDEN

MARIAN PAHARS
LATVIA

KAREL POBORSKY
CZECH REPUBLIC

PAULETA
PORTUGAL

LILIAN THURAM
FRANCE

GOT 10p FOR A CUPPA, GUV?

DON'T! Turn up looking like a tramp!

DAMN ITCHY BEARD!

DO! Make sure you have a shave beforehand!

PARP!

DON'T! Stand too near Alan 'Whiffy' Smiffy!

...AND TRAINING!

WHO THE HELL...

DON'T! Mistake training for ten-pin bowling!

DON'T! Run so fast Sven can't tell who you are!

CHECK IT!

THE OFFICIAL EURO 2004 BALL!

Check the ball they'll be using in Portugal this summer – the wicked Adidas Roteiro! David Beckham helped to test the ball in Madrid, so hopefully the practice will help him whip in a few free–kicks against France and the like! The ball is on sale now for £60, so watch out for it!

WHAT'S GOING ON IN THE MIND OF...

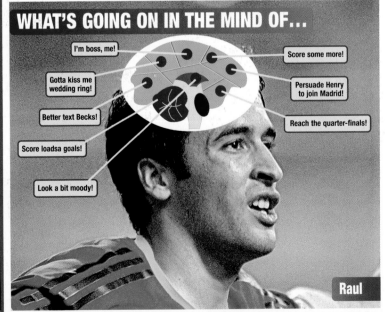

I'm boss, me!

Score some more!

Gotta kiss me wedding ring!

Persuade Henry to join Madrid!

Better text Becks!

Reach the quarter-finals!

Score loadsa goals!

Look a bit moody!

Raul

ENGLAND

★ THE QUALIFYING SQUAD ★

Goalkeepers

David James
Club: Man. City
Age: 33 ★ Caps/Goals: 22/0

Paul Robinson
Club: Leeds
Age: 24 ★ Caps/Goals: 4/0

Ian Walker
Club: Leicester
Age: 32 ★ Caps/Goals: 3/0

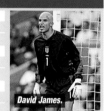
David James.

Defenders

Sol Campbell.

Danny Mills
Club: Leeds
Age: 27 ★ Caps/Goals: 19/0

Gary Neville
Club: Man. United
Age: 29 ★ Caps/Goals: 61/0

Phil Neville
Club: Man. United
Age: 27 ★ Caps/Goals: 45/0

Gareth Southgate
Club: Middlesbrough
Age: 33 ★ Caps/Goals: 56/2

Wayne Bridge
Club: Chelsea
Age: 23 ★ Caps/Goals: 16/0

John Terry
Club: Chelsea
Age: 23 ★ Caps/Goals: 6/0

Sol Campbell
Club: Arsenal
Age: 29 ★ Caps/Goals: 56/1

Matt Upson
Club: Birmingham
Age: 25 ★ Caps/Goals: 6/0

Ashley Cole
Club: Arsenal
Age: 23 ★ Caps/Goals: 24/0

Jonathan Woodgate
Club: Newcastle
Age: 24 ★ Caps/Goals: 4/0

Midfielders

David Beckham
Club: Real Madrid
Age: 29 ★ Caps/Goals: 66/13

Nicky Butt
Club: Man. United
Age: 29 ★ Caps/Goals: 32/0

Joe Cole
Club: Chelsea
Age: 22 ★ Caps/Goals: 14/2

Kieron Dyer
Club: Newcastle
Age: 25 ★ Caps/Goals: 20/0

Steven Gerrard
Club: Liverpool
Age: 24 ★ Caps/Goals: 21/3

Owen Hargreaves
Club: Bayern Munich
Age: 23 ★ Caps/Goals: 16/0

Jermaine Jenas
Club: Newcastle
Age: 21 ★ Caps/Goals: 5/0

Frank Lampard
Club: Chelsea
Age: 25 ★ Caps/Goals: 17/1

Danny Murphy
Club: Liverpool
Age: 27 ★ Caps/Goals: 9/1

Paul Scholes
Club: Man. United
Age: 29 ★ Caps/Goals: 60/13

Steven Gerrard.

Nicky Butt.

Strikers

Emile Heskey
Club: Liverpool
Age: 26 ★ Caps/Goals: 39/5

Michael Owen
Club: Liverpool
Age: 24 ★ Caps/Goals: 54/24

Wayne Rooney
Club: Everton
Age: 18 ★ Caps/Goals: 10/3

Alan Smith
Club: Leeds
Age: 23 ★ Caps/Goals: 7/1

Darius Vassell
Club: Aston Villa
Age: 23 ★ Caps/Goals: 15/4

Darius Vassell.

Wayne Rooney will scare the pants off defenders!

Sven Goran Eriksson's men are hungry for success, but can **ENGLAND** win Euro 2004?

HOW DID THEY QUALIFY?

England had a dodgy start to their Euro 2004 campaign – winning in Slovakia with just minutes left and then drawing 2-2 at home with Macedonia. That was David Seaman's last game for England, after he let in a goal direct from a corner. But Sven's men won their next five games and were brilliant in Turkey – carving out a 0-0 draw to finish ahead of the Turks and qualify automatically.

WHAT ARE ENGLAND'S STRENGTHS?

Apart from a top-class midfield and one of the most exciting youngsters in world football – Wayne Rooney – England's major strength is their team spirit, which is always important at major tournaments. Skipper David Beckham has a lot of respect in the squad, and Michael Owen, Paul Scholes and the boy Rooney are capable of terrorising any team!

AND THEIR WEAKNESSES?

Sven's got loads of midfielders, but the team is still unbalanced with no naturally left-sided player. Up front, only Michael Owen is guaranteed to score goals, so the whole of England needs to pray that the Liverpool striker stays fit! David James hasn't got any experience in international tournaments, but he was good in qualifying and if he starts well, he could become one of the surprise stars.

HOW WILL THEY DO?

If Sven has a full squad to choose from, England could go all the way – honestly! France and Italy might be favourites to win Euro 2004, but there's a real determination about this set of players – led by the inspirational David Beckham. There's a good mix of experienced internationals and young talent, and if the team makes a good start against France, we're backing the boys to bring the trophy home!

★ ENGLAND'S STRONGEST LINE-UP ★

JAMES

G NEVILLE | TERRY | CAMPBELL | A COLE

BECKHAM | BUTT | SCHOLES | GERRARD

OWEN | ROONEY

Will Becks and the Three Lions be roaring their way to victory at Euro 2004?

★ FINAL QUALIFYING TABLE ★

TEAM	P	W	D	L	F	A	PTS
1. ENGLAND	8	6	2	0	14	5	20
2. TURKEY	8	6	1	1	17	5	19
3. SLOVAKIA	8	3	1	4	11	9	10
4. MACEDONIA	8	1	3	4	11	14	6
5. LIECHTENSTEIN	8	0	1	7	2	22	1

England beat Slovakia 2-1 at The Riverside.

ENGLAND STATS & FACTS!

MANAGER: Sven Goran Eriksson
CAPTAIN: David Beckham
MOST CAPS (Current Squad): David Beckham, 66
MOST GOALS (Qualifying): David Beckham & Michael Owen, 5

WORLD RANKING: 8th
ODDS TO WIN EURO 2004: 8/1

PREVIOUS TOURNAMENTS
EURO 2000: Group Stages
BEST EVER: Semi-finals, 1996

★ ENGLAND'S STAR MEN ★

DAVID BECKHAM ★ Midfielder

It's time for David Beckham to dominate a tournament, and Euro 2004 could be the one. Playing in Spain with Real Madrid has opened his eyes, and he's a better player for leaving the Premiership. The captain's ability from free-kicks will frighten the life out of the opposition, and his amazing never-say-die attitude makes England a real threat.

PAUL SCHOLES ★ Midfielder

Under-rated in England, Paul Scholes is respected by some of the finest players in Europe – because they can't get near him! Scholesy keeps England ticking with a neat pass-and-move game that makes him very tricky to mark. And if you lose the Ginger Ninja in the box, you're asking for trouble!

MICHAEL OWEN ★ Striker

It's been a difficult season for Michael Owen at Liverpool, but he should have some extra energy after spending three months on the sidelines through injury. Little MO will relish playing with Beckham, Scholes, Gerrard and Rooney in the same team – and if they get the supply line right, Owen will do the rest!

★ WHO PLAYED IN ENGLAND'S EURO 2004 QUALIFYING GAMES? ★

SLOVAKIA		MACEDONIA		LIECHTENSTEIN		TURKEY		SLOVAKIA		MACEDONIA		LIECHTENSTEIN		TURKEY	
Won 2-1 (a)		Drew 2-2 (h)		Won 2-0 (a)		Won 2-0 (h)		Won 2-1 (h)		Won 2-1 (a)		Won 2-0 (h)		Drew 0-0 (a)	
Seaman		Seaman		James		James		James		James		James		James	
G Neville		G Neville		G Neville		G Neville		Mills		G Neville		G Neville		G Neville	
A Cole		A Cole		Bridge		Bridge		A Cole		A Cole		A Cole		A Cole	
Woodgate		Woodgate		Ferdinand		Ferdinand		Upson		Terry		Terry		Terry	
Southgate		Campbell		Southgate		Campbell		Southgate		Campbell		Upson		Campbell	
Gerrard		Gerrard 1		Gerrard		Gerrard		Gerrard		Hargreaves		Gerrard		Gerrard	
Beckham 1		Beckham 1		Beckham 1		Beckham 1		Beckham 1		Beckham 1		Beckham		Beckham	
Scholes		Scholes		Scholes		Scholes		Scholes		Lampard		Lampard		Lampard	
Butt		Bridge		Dyer		Butt		P Neville		Scholes		Rooney 1		Butt	
Heskey		Smith		Heskey		Rooney		Rooney		P Neville		Beattie		Rooney	
Owen 1		Owen		Owen 1		Owen		Owen 2		Rooney 1		Owen 1		Heskey	
Substitutes:		*Substitutes:*		*Substitutes:*		*Substitutes:*		*Substitutes:*		Owen		*Substitutes:*		*Substitutes:*	
Dyer	77	Butt	54	Butt	65	Vassell 1	58	Hargreaves	43	*Substitutes:*		Hargreaves	58	Vassell	69
Hargreaves	86	Vassell	59	Murphy	70	Dyer	89	Vassell	57	Heskey	46	P Neville	58	Dyer	73
Smith	90			Rooney	80					P Neville	74	J Cole	70	Lampard	90
								Dyer	86	J Cole	70				

John Terry.

MATCHMAN'S VERDICT!

"We luv ya England, we do! Look, I 'as 'ad a chat wiv Sven's boys and dey recks we is gonna surprise everyone by winning da trophy – wiv Rooney a biggedy star!"

GROUP B

ENGLAND

FRANCE

SWITZERLAND

CROATIA

FRANCE

France won the tournament in 2000 and are favourites again.

The European Champions will be going all-out to keep their title.

★ THE QUALIFYING SQUAD ★

Goalkeepers

Fabien Barthez
Club: Man. United
Age: 32 ★ Caps/Goals: 64/0

Grégory Coupet
Club: Lyon
Age: 31 ★ Caps/Goals: 4/0

Mickaël Landreau
Club: Nantes
Age: 25 ★ Caps/Goals: 2/0

Fabien Barthez.

Defenders

William Gallas.

Marcel Desailly
Club: Chelsea
Age: 35 ★ Caps/Goals: 112/3

William Gallas
Club: Chelsea
Age: 26 ★ Caps/Goals: 9/0

Bixente Lizarazu
Club: Bayern Munich
Age: 34 ★ Caps/Goals: 91/2

Jean-Alain Boumsong
Club: Rangers
Age: 24 ★ Caps/Goals: 2/0

Jérémie Bréchet
Club: Inter Milan
Age: 24 ★ Caps/Goals: 3/0

Vincent Candela
Club: Roma
Age: 30 ★ Caps/Goals: 40/2

Philippe Christanval
Club: Marseille
Age: 25 ★ Caps/Goals: 4/0

Philippe Mexes
Club: Auxerre
Age: 22 ★ Caps/Goals: 6/0

Willy Sagnol
Club: Bayern Munich
Age: 27 ★ Caps/Goals: 20/0

Mikaël Silvestre
Club: Man. United
Age: 26 ★ Caps/Goals: 27/2

Lilian Thuram
Club: Juventus
Age: 32 ★ Caps/Goals: 95/2

Midfielders

Eric Carrière
Club: Lyon
Age: 31 ★ Caps/Goals: 10/5

Olivier Kapo
Club: Auxerre
Age: 23 ★ Caps/Goals: 8/3

Olivier Dacourt
Club: Roma
Age: 29 ★ Caps/Goals: 10/0

Ludovic Giuly
Club: Monaco
Age: 27 ★ Caps/Goals: 5/1

Claude Makelele
Club: Chelsea
Age: 31 ★ Caps/Goals: 28/0

Olivier Dacourt.

Benoît Pedretti
Club: Sochaux
Age: 23 ★ Caps/Goals: 7/0

Robert Pires
Club: Arsenal
Age: 31 ★ Caps/Goals: 67/14

Jérôme Rothen
Club: Monaco
Age: 26 ★ Caps/Goals: 4/0

Patrick Vieira
Club: Arsenal
Age: 27 ★ Caps/Goals: 66/4

Zinedine Zidane
Club: Real Madrid
Age: 31 ★ Caps/Goals: 87/22

Jérôme Rothen.

Strikers

Sidney Govou
Club: Lyon
Age: 24 ★ Caps/Goals: 10/3

Thierry Henry
Club: Arsenal
Age: 26 ★ Caps/Goals: 55/25

Steve Marlet
Club: Fulham
Age: 30 ★ Caps/Goals: 21/5

Louis Saha
Club: Man. United
Age: 25 ★ Caps/Goals: 1/1

David Trezeguet
Club: Juventus
Age: 26 ★ Caps/Goals: 48/28

Sylvain Wiltord
Club: Arsenal
Age: 30 ★ Caps/Goals: 59/20

David Trezeguet.

Will FRANCE put the disappointment of the World Cup behind them to win another trophy?

HOW DID THEY QUALIFY?

France qualified in style! They won all eight of their games, scoring an incredible 29 goals and conceding just two! And having to qualify for Euro 2004 by playing competitive games will make Les Bleus a lot more prepared than they were for the 2002 World Cup – when they qualified automatically as holders. That meant they looked very rusty in South Korea & Japan, but they look absolutely unstoppable going into this competition.

WHAT ARE FRANCE'S STRENGTHS?

There's experience all through the team – the defence is solid and they're protected by the awesome Patrick Vieira and Claude Makelele. Zinedine Zidane is the best player in the world, Robert Pires will be raring to go after missing the World Cup, and Henry and Trezeguet are two of the best strikers on the planet. Not bad, eh?

AND THEIR WEAKNESSES?

Fabien Barthez is a shadow of the 'keeper he once was. After falling out of favour at Man. United he moved to Marseille on loan, but he became an unpopular figure with the fans. Bixente Lizarazu can also be a weak link in defence, but France are still a world-class team and they know each other well. They didn't even need to experiment in qualifying, but if injury hits the squad, they've still got quality on the bench.

HOW WILL THEY DO?

Well, France were favourites to win the 2002 World Cup, but they fell at the first hurdle with a squad of very tired, over-confident players. But that experience should help Jacques Santini's men to focus on one game at a time. They won the Confederations Cup last summer and they've got the best squad in this competition. If they can beat England in the first game, they could hang on to the trophy!

★ FRANCE'S STRONGEST LINE-UP ★

BARTHEZ

THURAM — DESAILLY — GALLAS — LIZARAZU

PIRES — VIEIRA — MAKELELE — ZIDANE

TREZEGUET — HENRY

★ FINAL QUALIFYING TABLE ★

TEAM	P	W	D	L	F	A	PTS
1. FRANCE	8	8	0	0	29	2	24
2. SLOVENIA	8	4	2	2	15	12	14
3. ISRAEL	8	2	3	3	9	11	9
4. CYPRUS	8	2	2	4	9	18	8
5. MALTA	8	0	1	7	5	24	1

France ripped it up in qualifying!

FRANCE STATS & FACTS!

MANAGER: Jacques Santini

CAPTAIN: Marcel Desailly

MOST CAPS (Current Squad):
Marcel Desailly, 112

MOST GOALS (Qualifying):
Henry, Trezeguet & Wiltord, 6

WORLD RANKING: 2nd

ODDS TO WIN EURO 2004: 4/1

PREVIOUS TOURNAMENTS

EURO 2000: Winners

BEST EVER: Winners, 1984 & 2000

★ FRANCE'S STAR MEN ★

PATRICK VIEIRA ★ Midfielder

One of the best midfielders in world football, it's no surprise to learn that Real Madrid are desperate to sign Patrick Vieira as soon as possible. The Arsenal star loves playing just in front of Claude Makelele for the European champs, and he's an impossible man to stop when he starts a run with those huge legs!

ZINEDINE ZIDANE ★ Midfielder

The Real Madrid genius was injured for the first two games of the 2002 World Cup and France missed his creative talents badly. Zidane will be the trickiest playmaker in the tournament – and England will need to keep the World Player Of The Year as quiet as possible in the opening game of Group B!

THIERRY HENRY ★ Striker

There isn't a striker in the world who can compete with Henry's all-round game. The Arsenal star combines awesome ball control with breathtaking pace, and his finishing has improved dramatically in the last two years. Titi has also become a master of free-kicks and setting up his team-mates with assists – all in all, he's a defender's nightmare!

★ WHO PLAYED IN FRANCE'S EURO 2004 QUALIFYING GAMES? ★

CYPRUS		SLOVENIA		MALTA		MALTA		ISRAEL		CYPRUS		SLOVENIA		ISRAEL	
Won 2-1 (a)		Won 5-0 (h)		Won 4-0 (a)		Won 6-0 (h)		Won 2-1 (a)		Won 5-0 (h)		Won 2-0 (a)		Won 3-0 (h)	
Coupet		Barthez		Barthez		Barthez		Barthez		Barthez		Barthez		Barthez	
Thuram		Thuram		Thuram		Thuram		Thuram		Thuram		Thuram		Thuram	
Silvestre		Silvestre		Silvestre		Lizarazu		Lizarazu		Lizarazu		Lizarazu		Lizarazu	
Christanval		Gallas		Gallas		Gallas		Gallas		Silvestre		Silvestre		Boumsong	1
Desailly		Desailly		Desailly		Silvestre		Silvestre		Desailly		Desailly		Reveillere	
Makelele		Makelele		Makelele		Makelele		Makelele		Makelele		Makelele		Dacourt	
Vieira		Vieira		Vieira	1	Pedretti		Vieira		Vieira		Vieira		Pedretti	
Zidane		Zidane		Zidane		Zidane	2	Zidane	1	Pires		Zidane		Zidane	
Wiltord	1	Wiltord	1	Wiltord	1	Wiltord	1	Wiltord		Wiltord	2	Wiltord		Pires	
Cisse	1	Henry		Henry	2	Henry	2	Henry		Henry	1	Henry		Henry	1
Marlet		Marlet	2	Marlet		Trezeguet	1	Trezeguet	1	Trezeguet	2	Trezeguet	1	Trezeguet	1
Substitutes:		*Substitutes:*		*Substitutes:*		*Substitutes:*		*Substitutes:*		*Substitutes:*		*Substitutes:*		*Substitutes:*	
Govou	70	Cheyrou	80	Dacourt	70	Sagnol	66	Govou	66	Sagnol	64	Sagnol	77	Cissé	78
Kapo	81	Govou	1 80	Carrière	1 78	Govou	74	Cisse	74	Dacourt	70	Pires	81	Giuly	85
		Sagnol	84	Mexes	85	Rothen	81			Marlet	77	Dacourt	1 70	Marlet	85

Bixente Lizarazu.

SWITZERLAND

★ THE QUALIFYING SQUAD ★

Goalkeepers

Fabrice Borer
Club: Grasshoppers
Age: 32 ★ Caps/Goals: 3/0

Jörg Stiel
Club: Borussia Monchengladbach
Age: 36 ★ Caps/Goals: 14/0

Pascal Zuberbühler
Club: FC Basle
Age: 33 ★ Caps/Goals: 18/0

Jörg Stiel.

Defenders

Christoph Spycher.

Bruno Berner
Club: Grasshoppers
Age: 26 ★ Caps/Goals: 12/0

Bernt Haas
Club: West Brom
Age: 26 ★ Caps/Goals: 24/3

Stéphane Henchoz
Club: Liverpool
Age: 29 ★ Caps/Goals: 61/0

Stephan Keller
Club: FC Zurich
Age: 25 ★ Caps/Goals: 0/0

Ludovic Magnin
Club: Werder Bremen
Age: 25 ★ Caps/Goals: 11/1

Remo Meyer
Club: 1860 Munich
Age: 23 ★ Caps/Goals: 4/0

Patrick Müller
Club: Lyon
Age: 27 ★ Caps/Goals: 41/2

Alain Rochat
Club: BSC Young Boys
Age: 21 ★ Caps/Goals: 0/0

Christoph Spycher
Club: Grasshoppers
Age: 26 ★ Caps/Goals: 3/0

Murat Yakin
Club: FC Basle
Age: 29 ★ Caps/Goals: 40/4

Marco Zwyssig
Club: FC Basle
Age: 32 ★ Caps/Goals: 18/1

Midfielders

Ricardo Cabanas
Club: Grasshoppers
Age: 25 ★ Caps/Goals: 11/2

Mario Cantaluppi
Club: FC Basle
Age: 30 ★ Caps/Goals: 12/0

Fabio Celestini
Club: Marseille
Age: 28 ★ Caps/Goals: 23/1

Sébastien Fournier
Club: Servette
Age: 32 ★ Caps/Goals: 12/1

Benjamin Huggel
Club: FC Basle
Age: 26 ★ Caps/Goals: 3/0

Fabio Celestini.

Massimo Lombardo
Club: Servette
Age: 31 ★ Caps/Goals: 8/0

Johann Vogel
Club: PSV Eindhoven
Age: 27 ★ Caps/Goals: 61/2

Raphael Wicky
Club: Hamburg
Age: 27 ★ Caps/Goals: 47/0

Hakan Yakin
Club: Stuttgart
Age: 27 ★ Caps/Goals: 27/11

Johann Vogel.

Strikers

Stéphane Chapuisat
Club: BSC Young Boys
Age: 34 ★ Caps/Goals: 96/21

Alexander Frei
Club: Rennes
Age: 24 ★ Caps/Goals: 22/14

Mailaim Rama
Club: FC Thun
Age: 28 ★ Caps/Goals: 3/0

Marco Streller
Club: Stuttgart
Age: 22 ★ Caps/Goals: 0/0

Léonard Thurre
Club: Servette
Age: 27 ★ Caps/Goals: 4/0

Marco Streller.

The Swiss beat the Republic Of Ireland twice during qualifying.

Stephane Chapuisat scored against England at Euro '96!

They're the underdogs in a tough Group B, but SWITZERLAND would love to cause an upset!

HOW DID THEY QUALIFY?

Switzerland started their campaign with a 4-1 hammering of Georgia, but their best result in qualifying was a 2-1 away victory in Dublin, which prompted Mick McCarthy to resign as the Republic Of Ireland manager. With two games to go, the Swiss lost 4-1 to a Russia side badly needing points – but they still finished top of the group after beating the Republic 2-0 at home in the final match.

WHAT ARE SWITZERLAND'S STRENGTHS?

Coach Köbi Kuhn has created an attacking side that's capable of scoring goals – something of a problem for Switzerland in past campaigns. Their best player is midfield trickster Hakan Yakin, who makes the side tick playing behind the two strikers – veteran Stéphane Chapuisat and exciting young Rennes striker Alexander Frei.

AND THEIR WEAKNESSES?

Switzerland conceded 11 goals in their eight qualifying games, and their midfield often features three attack-minded midfielders – Hakan Yakin, Raphael Wicky and Ricardo Cabanas. This leaves Johann Vogel with a big job to do in protecting the defence, so they could struggle against teams that defend well and attack quickly on the break. They'll have to be especially careful when they face France and England – with the frightening pace of Thierry Henry and Michael Owen.

HOW WILL THEY DO?

Well, Switzerland got some good results in qualifying – and they've got two very talented individuals in Hakan Yakin and Frei. But that probably won't be good enough to upset the leading teams in Group B – and the Swiss haven't got a brilliant record in the European Championships. They've only qualified once before, in 1996, and they'll do well just to finish above Croatia in the group stages.

★ SWITZERLAND'S STRONGEST LINE-UP ★

STIEL

HAAS — M YAKIN — MÜLLER — MAGNIN

VOGEL

CABANAS — H YAKIN — WICKY

CHAPUISAT — FREI

★ FINAL QUALIFYING TABLE ★

TEAM	P	W	D	L	F	A	PTS
1. SWITZERLAND	8	4	3	1	15	11	15
2. RUSSIA	8	4	2	2	19	12	14
3. REP. OF IRELAND	8	3	2	3	10	11	11
4. ALBANIA	8	2	2	4	11	15	8
5. GEORGIA	8	2	1	5	8	14	7

The Swiss celebrate after qualifying for Euro 2004.

SWITZERLAND STATS & FACTS!

MANAGER: Köbi Kuhn

CAPTAIN: Jörg Stiel

MOST CAPS (Current Squad):
Stephane Chapuisat, 96

MOST GOALS (Qualifying):
Alexander Frei, 5

WORLD RANKING: 44th

ODDS TO WIN EURO 2004: 100/1

PREVIOUS TOURNAMENTS

EURO 2000: Did Not Qualify

BEST EVER: 1996, Group Stages

★ SWITZERLAND'S STAR MEN ★

MURAT YAKIN ★ Defender

Murat Yakin isn't a fancy player – he's the kind of old-fashioned defender who prefers to boot clearances into Row Z! But he's an experienced international and an excellent organiser at the back. The 29-year-old Basle veteran also takes Switzerland's set-pieces, and scored during qualifying against Albania.

HAKAN YAKIN ★ Midfielder

Hakan Yakin, younger brother of Murat, plays in the hole behind Switzerland's two strikers – dancing his way through the tackles and causing havoc in opposition defences with his pace and skill. The Stuttgart star is an intelligent player, and England's midfielders will have to stop his clever passing and late bursts into the box to avoid an upset!

ALEXANDER FREI ★ Striker

This 24-year-old striker could cause a shock in Group B. He scored five times in qualifying and he's got an excellent international record, with ten goals in his last 13 appearances. Frei hasn't set the French league alight since moving to Rennes last year, but he's strong in the air and a real handful for defenders.

★ WHO PLAYED IN SWITZERLAND'S EURO 2004 QUALIFYING GAMES? ★

GEORGIA	ALBANIA	REP. OF IRE	GEORGIA	RUSSIA	ALBANIA	RUSSIA	REP. OF IRE
Won 4-1 (h)	Drew 1-1 (a)	Won 2-1 (a)	Drew 0-0 (a)	Drew 2-2 (h)	Won 3-2 (h)	Lost 4-1 (a) *og	Won 2-0 (h)
Stiel	Stiel	Stiel	Zuberbühler	Stiel	Stiel	Zuberbuehler	Stiel
Haas	Haas	Haas	Haas	Haas	Haas 1	Meyer	Haas
Magnin	Magnin	Magnin	Berner	Magnin	Berner	Berner	Spycher
Muller 1	Muller	Muller	Meyer	Muller	Henchoz	Muller	Muller
M Yakin	M Yakin 1	M Yakin	M Yakin	M Yakin	M Yakin	M Yakin	M Yakin
Henchoz	Vogel	Vogel	Vogel	Celestini	Vogel	Henchoz	Vogel
Vogel	Cabanas	Cabanas	Cabanas	Cabanas	Cabanas 1	Vogel	Huggel
Cabanas	Wicky	Wicky	Wicky	Wicky	Wicky	Cabanas	Wicky
H Yakin 1	H Yakin	H Yakin	H Yakin	H Yakin	H Yakin	Celestini	H Yakin 1
Chapuisat 1	Chapuisat	Chapuisat	Chapuisat	Chapuisat	Chapuisat	Chapuisat	Chapuisat
Frei 1	Frei	Frei	Frei	Frei 2	Frei 1	Frei	Frei 1
Substitutes:	Substitutes:	Substitutes:	Substitutes:	Substitutes:	Substitutes:	Substitutes:	Substitutes:
Celestini 68	Celestini 63	Celestini 1 84	Celestini 59	Berner 60	Spycher 64	Huggel 63	Celestini 55
Wicky 73	Cantaluppi 80	Cantaluppi 84	Cantaluppi 67	Vogel 70	Zwyssig 75	Wicky 70	
Berner 82	Thurre 84			Henchoz 83	Celestini 83	Rama 78	

Raphael Wicky.

MATCHMAN'S VERDICT!

"I 'as been windin' up me wicked mate Hakan Yakin for months about da Swiss cheeses gettin' thrashed by England! You'll be fourth in dis group – soz, Hakan dude!"

CROATIA

★ THE QUALIFYING SQUAD ★

Goalkeepers

Tomislav Butina
Club: Club Brugge
Age: 30 ★ Caps/Goals: 10/0

Stipe Pletikosa
Club: Shakhtar Donetsk
Age: 25 ★ Caps/Goals: 38/0

Vedran Runje
Club: Marseille
Age: 28 ★ Caps/Goals: 0/0

Stipe Pletikosa.

Defenders

Stjepan Tomas.

Anthony Seric
Club: Brescia
Age: 24 ★ Caps/Goals: 11/0

Dario Simic
Club: AC Milan
Age: 28 ★ Caps/Goals: 63/2

Josip Simunic
Club: Hertha Berlin
Age: 26 ★ Caps/Goals: 20/1

Mario Tokic
Club: Grazer AK
Age: 28 ★ Caps/Goals: 10/0

Robert Kovac
Club: Bayern Munich
Age: 30 ★ Caps/Goals: 34/0

Stjepan Tomas
Club: Fenerbahce
Age: 28 ★ Caps/Goals: 33/1

Miljenko Mumlek
Club: Standard Liege
Age: 31 ★ Caps/Goals: 8/1

Igor Tudor
Club: Juventus
Age: 26 ★ Caps/Goals: 33/0

Mato Neretljak
Club: Hajduk Split
Age: 24 ★ Caps/Goals: 3/1

Boris Zivkovic
Club: Stuttgart
Age: 28 ★ Caps/Goals: 32/2

Midfielders

Jasmin Agic
Club: Dynamo Zagreb
Age: 29 ★ Caps/Goals: 12/0

Niko Kovac
Club: Hertha Berlin
Age: 32 ★ Caps/Goals: 34/6

Marko Babic
Club: Bayer Leverkusen
Age: 23 ★ Caps/Goals: 12/0

Jerko Leko
Club: Dynamo Kiev
Age: 24 ★ Caps/Goals: 15/1

Ivica Mornar
Club: Portsmouth
Age: 30 ★ Caps/Goals: 14/1

Milan Rapaic
Club: Ancona
Age: 30 ★ Caps/Goals: 39/5

Jerko Leko.

Giovani Rosso
Club: Maccabi Haifa
Age: 31 ★ Caps/Goals: 12/1

Darijo Srna
Club: Shakhtar Donetsk
Age: 22 ★ Caps/Goals: 13/1

Jurica Vranjes
Club: Stuttgart
Age: 24 ★ Caps/Goals: 12/0

Strikers

Bosko Balaban
Club: Club Brugge
Age: 25 ★ Caps/Goals: 15/6

Tomislav Sokota
Club: Benfica
Age: 27 ★ Caps/Goals: 1/0

Ivan Klasnic
Club: Werder Bremen
Age: 24 ★ Caps/Goals: 1/0

Davor Vugrinec
Club: Atalanta
Age: 29 ★ Caps/Goals: 26/7

Marijo Maric
Club: FC Karnten
Age: 27 ★ Caps/Goals: 7/1

Tomislav Maric
Club: Borussia Monchengladbach
Age: 31 ★ Caps/Goals: 9/2

Ivica Olic
Club: CSKA Moscow
Age: 24 ★ Caps/Goals: 19/4

Dado Prso
Club: Monaco
Age: 29 ★ Caps/Goals: 10/3

Marijo Maric.

Croatia are strong in defence and dangerous on the break.

CROATIA *will be one of the most determined teams at Euro 2004, but will that be enough?*

HOW DID THEY QUALIFY?

Croatia had a bad start – drawing against Estonia and then losing to Bulgaria. But they won their next four games and finished second in their group because of a better record in their two games against Belgium. Drawn with neighbouring country Slovenia in the play-offs, they qualified thanks to Monaco striker Dado Prso – who scored twice in a 2-1 aggregate win.

WHAT ARE CROATIA'S STRENGTHS?

Otto Baric's side only conceded five goals in qualifying, and Juventus star Igor Tudor is the rock in a well organised defence. There are plenty of options up front – with Prso, Ivica Olic, Marijo Maric and Bosko Balaban all competing for places – and they're determined to make an impression.

AND THEIR WEAKNESSES?

The midfield doesn't look strong enough and could struggle against world-class opponents like Patrick Vieira, Zinedine Zidane and David Beckham. Milan Rapaic is one of their key midfielders, but even he struggled to find a top European club when his contract ended at Fenerbahce last year. A general lack of experience in the squad could also prove important when the going gets tough.

HOW WILL THEY DO?

It depends on which Croatia turns up! They can destroy teams with their firepower – like in qualifying when they thrashed Belgium 4-0. But this team doesn't always travel well – and they failed to impress in a friendly against England last year. Drawn against France and England, they'll need to be in amazing form to reach the second round. More likely to battle with Switzerland for third place.

★ CROATIA'S STRONGEST LINE-UP ★

PLETIKOSA

ZIVKOVIC — TUDOR — R KOVAC — SIMUNIC

SRNA — N KOVAC — ROSSO — RAPAIC

PRSO — OLIC

★ FINAL QUALIFYING TABLE ★

TEAM	P	W	D	L	F	A	PTS
1. BULGARIA	8	5	2	1	13	4	17
2. CROATIA	8	5	1	2	12	4	16
3. BELGIUM	8	5	1	2	11	9	16
4. ESTONIA	8	2	2	4	4	6	8
5. ANDORRA	8	0	0	8	1	18	0

Croatia finished runners-up behind Bulgaria in qualifying.

CROATIA STATS & FACTS!

MANAGER: Otto Baric

CAPTAIN: Boris Zivkovic

MOST CAPS (Current Squad):
Dario Simic, 63

MOST GOALS (Qualifying):
Dado Prso, 3

WORLD RANKING: 20th

ODDS TO WIN EURO 2004: 80/1

PREVIOUS TOURNAMENTS

EURO 2000: Did Not Qualify

BEST EVER: Quarter-finals, 1996

★ CROATIA'S STAR MEN ★

IGOR TUDOR ★ Defender

The tall, powerful Juventus defender missed the World Cup in South Korea & Japan and has struggled with injury again this season, but he should be on the plane to Portugal in June. He's a real leader at the back and always looks dangerous from set-pieces, so his fitness is crucial to Croatia's hopes.

DADO PRSO ★ Striker

It's taken a while for Dado Prso to get his footy career on track, but he goes into this tournament as one of Europe's most in-form strikers. The 29-year-old Croatian Player Of The Year bagged an amazing four goals in Monaco's record 8-3 win over Deportivo in the Champions League – and he scored twice in the play-off games against Slovenia.

IVICA OLIC ★ Striker

Olic shot to fame when he scored in Croatia's shock 2-1 win over Italy at the 2002 World Cup. The 24-year-old star was top scorer in the Croatian league for two consecutive seasons before moving to CSKA Moscow, and this tournament could be his chance to secure a switch to one of Europe's top clubs.

MATCHMAN'S VERDICT!

"I 'as big respect for Croatia and their mad-lookin' shirts! Hopefully they'll be duff against England but I'll support 'em against France!"

★ WHO PLAYED IN CROATIA'S EURO 2004 QUALIFYING GAMES? ★

ESTONIA	BULGARIA	BELGIUM	ANDORRA	ESTONIA	ANDORRA	BELGIUM	BULGARIA	SLOVENIA	SLOVENIA
Drew 0-0 (h)	*Lost 2-0 (a)*	*Won 4-0 (h)*	*Won 2-0 (h)*	*Won 1-0 (a)*	*Won 3-0 (a)*	*Lost 2-1 (a)*	*Won 1-0 (h)*	*Drew 1-1 (h)*	*Won 1-0 (a)*
Pletikosa	Pletikosa	Pletikosa	Pletikosa	Pletikosa	Pletikosa	Pletikosa	Pletikosa	Pletikosa	Pletikosa
D Simic	D Simic	D Simic	D Simic	D Simic	D Simic	D Simic 1	D Simic	D Simic	Zivkovic
Tapalovic	Zivkovic	Simunic	Simunic	Simunic	Simunic 1	Simunic	Zivkovic	Neretljak	Simunic
Tokic	Tudor	Tudor	Tudor	Tomas	Tomas	Tomas	Tudor	Tudor	R Kovac
S Maric	Tomas	R Kovac	R Kovac	Zivkovic	R Kovac	R Kovac	R Kovac	Tomas	N Kovac
Saric	N Kovac	Zivkovic	Zivkovic	N Kovac 1	N Kovac 1	Zivkovic	Vranjes	Zivkovic	Srna
Babic	Leko	Srna 1	Srna	Srna	Leko	Leko	Srna	Leko	Rapaic
Vugrinec	Stanic	Rosso	Leko	Babic	Rosso 1	Rosso	Leko	Mornar	Rosso
Olic	Rapaic	Rapaic	Rapaic 2	Rapaic	Rapaic	Rapaic	Rapaic	Prso 1	Prso 1
T Maric	Vugrinec	Prso 1	Prso	Prso	Mornar	Mornar	Mornar	Olic	Sokota
	Boksic	T Maric 1	T Maric	Olic	Olic	Olic	Prso		
Substitutes:	*Substitutes:*	*Substitutes:*	*Substitutes:*	*Substitutes:*	*Substitutes:*	*Substitutes:*	*Substitutes:*	*Substitutes:*	*Substitutes:*
Rapaic 46	Olic 45	Leko 1 46	Stanic 46	T Maric 61	Vranjes 32	Prso 46	Olic 1 46	Rapajic 46	Babic 53
Petric 60	S Maric 46	Stanic 70	N Kovac 47	Leko 74	Tudor 46	Srna 62	Babic 54	Rosso 46	Tomas 66
Tomas 79		N Kovac 76	Babic 65	Rosso 80	Prso 57	M Maric 77	Rosso 76	Srna 59	Leko 75

STOP PRESS...STOP PRESS...STOP PRESS...
Back in Euro 2000, top France striker Nicolas Anelka tipped Louis Saha as the next big thing. But the Man. United ace is now keeping Anelka out of France's squad for Euro 2004! Gutted, Nico!

NON, NON, NON! SAHA IS RUBBISH, GAFFER!

210

It took 210 games and 43 to cut down the 50 teams Euro 2004 qualifying sta the 15 who are joining Po in the finals this s

A RECENT HISTORY OF

ENGLAND'S

Salt 'n' Lineker flavour rocks!

1 At Euro '88 in West Germany, England had Gary Lineker firing…

No more crisps for you lot!

4 By Euro '92, star striker Lineker was being subbed…

Help me! there's superglue on this bloomin' thing!

7 …who amazingly beat Germany in the final to win the cup!

MEET THE FANS!

GERMANY OH DEAR!

GREECE BIG HEADS!

CZECH REPUBLIC TOP TUNES!

FRANCE PASSIONATE!

SWEDEN GIRLY!

DENMARK BONKERS!

PORTUGAL LOUD!

CROATIA BALDIES!

SWITZERLAND RED-FACED!

ITALY SCARY!

BULGARIA TIRED!

HOLLAND CONFUSED!

10 …but Gareth Southgate's missed penalty sent England out…

Mummy, I've got no hair on me chest! Wah, wah, wah!

13 …but France started the tournament in brilliant form…

ITALY

★ THE QUALIFYING SQUAD ★

Goalkeepers

Christian Abbiati
Club: AC Milan
Age: 26 ★ Caps/Goals: 2/0

Gianluigi Buffon
Club: Juventus
Age: 26 ★ Caps/Goals: 42/0

Francesco Toldo
Club: Inter Milan
Age: 32 ★ Caps/Goals: 28/0

Gianluigi Buffon.

Defenders

Fabio Cannavaro.

Nicola Legrottaglie
Club: Juventus
Age: 27 ★ Caps/Goals: 7/1

Alessandro Nesta
Club: AC Milan
Age: 28 ★ Caps/Goals: 56/0

Massimo Oddo
Club: Lazio
Age: 27 ★ Caps/Goals: 10/0

Christian Panucci
Club: Roma
Age: 31 ★ Caps/Goals: 41/2

Fabio Cannavaro
Club: Inter Milan
Age: 30 ★ Caps/Goals: 75/0

Gianluca Zambrotta
Club: Juventus
Age: 27 ★ Caps/Goals: 35/0

Matteo Ferrari
Club: Parma
Age: 24 ★ Caps/Goals: 8/0

Luciano Zauri
Club: Lazio
Age: 26 ★ Caps/Goals: 5/0

Midfielders

Massimo Ambrosini
Club: AC Milan
Age: 27 ★ Caps/Goals: 19/0

Mauro Camoranesi
Club: Juventus
Age: 27 ★ Caps/Goals: 6/0

Stefano Fiore
Club: Lazio
Age: 29 ★ Caps/Goals: 30/2

Francesco Totti.

Gennaro Gattuso
Club: AC Milan
Age: 26 ★ Caps/Goals: 23/1

Andrea Pirlo
Club: AC Milan
Age: 25 ★ Caps/Goals: 6/0

Simone Perrotta
Club: Chievo
Age: 26 ★ Caps/Goals: 13/0

Alessio Tacchinardi
Club: Juventus
Age: 28 ★ Caps/Goals: 13/0

Simone Perrotta.

Damiano Tommasi
Club: Roma
Age: 30 ★ Caps/Goals: 24/1

Francesco Totti
Club: Roma
Age: 27 ★ Caps/Goals: 38/6

Cristiano Zanetti
Club: Inter Milan
Age: 27 ★ Caps/Goals: 15/1

Strikers

Antonio Cassano
Club: Roma
Age: 21 ★ Caps/Goals: 2/1

Fabrizio Miccoli
Club: Juventus
Age: 24 ★ Caps/Goals: 5/0

Bernardo Corradi
Club: Lazio
Age: 28 ★ Caps/Goals: 8/2

Christian Vieri
Club: Inter Milan
Age: 30 ★ Caps/Goals: 37/20

Alessandro del Piero
Club: Juventus
Age: 29 ★ Caps/Goals: 62/23

Marco Delvecchio
Club: Roma
Age: 31 ★ Caps/Goals: 21/4

Marco di Vaio
Club: Juventus
Age: 27 ★ Caps/Goals: 10/2

Filippo Inzaghi
Club: AC Milan
Age: 30 ★ Caps/Goals: 47/20

Fabrizio Miccoli.

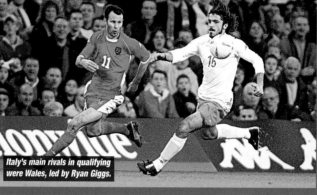
Italy's main rivals in qualifying were Wales, led by Ryan Giggs.

ITALY were beaten finalists at Euro 2000, so nothing less than victory will do in Portugal!

HOW DID THEY QUALIFY?

Italy's footballers like to make life hard and they made a slow start. After a 2-0 win against minnows Azerbaijan, Italy drew at home against Serbia & Montenegro then lost in Wales. Form was patchy, so coach Giovanni Trapattoni tinkered with his formation and brought in some fresh faces – and the team fought back with successive 2-0 wins over Finland before a 4-0 home victory over Wales saw them win the group.

WHAT ARE ITALY'S STRENGTHS?

Trapattoni has lots of good options in attack. Christian Vieri is the main centre-forward, but he's supported by Francesco Totti and Alessandro Del Piero in an awesome line-up. Then there's Inzaghi, Di Vaio, Corradi, Miccoli and new star Cassano all offering support!

AND THEIR WEAKNESSES?

As Italy showed in the 2002 World Cup, if their first-choice defence is broken up, they can look shaky. The centre-back partnership of Fabio Cannavaro and Alessandro Nesta is as strong as any – but if injury or suspension strikes, the back-up is inexperienced. Matteo Ferrari and Nicola Legrottaglie are good prospects, but they haven't played much international football. That's only a small criticism, though. Overall, Italy don't have many weaknesses!

HOW WILL THEY DO?

Only a last-minute France goal denied Italy victory at Euro 2000, and this squad is a better bet to win the tournament – especially as Trapattoni has found a way to include the golden trio of Del Piero, Totti and Vieri in his starting line-up. Group C shouldn't provide too many problems, and if Italy continue their positive approach to matches, they could really make an impact.

★ ITALY'S STRONGEST LINE-UP ★

BUFFON

ODDO — CANNAVARO — NESTA — ZAMBROTTA

ZANETTI — PERROTTA

CAMORANESI — TOTTI — DEL PIERO

VIERI

★ FINAL QUALIFYING TABLE ★

TEAM	P	W	D	L	F	A	PTS
1. ITALY	8	5	2	1	17	4	17
2. WALES	8	4	1	3	13	10	13
3. SERBIA & MONTENEGRO	8	3	3	2	11	11	12
4. FINLAND	8	3	1	4	9	10	10
5. AZERBAIJAN	8	1	1	6	5	20	4

Italy topped their group by four points.

ITALY STATS & FACTS!

MANAGER: Giovanni Trapattoni

CAPTAIN: Fabio Cannavaro

MOST CAPS (Current Squad):
Fabio Cannavaro, 75

MOST GOALS (Qualifying):
Filippo Inzaghi, 6

WORLD RANKING: 10th

ODDS TO WIN EURO 2004: 5/1

PREVIOUS TOURNAMENTS

EURO 2000: Runners-up

BEST EVER: Winners, 1968

★ ITALY'S STAR MEN ★

GIANLUCA ZAMBROTTA ★ Defender

When Zambrotta returned to Italy's line-up in qualifying, it was no fluke that results started to improve. The Juventus star started his career as a right-winger but has transformed himself into a top left-back, and his attacking runs have given Italy a new dimension. After a red card in the Euro 2000 semi-final, he'll want to make the right headlines in Portgual.

ALESSANDRO DEL PIERO ★ Striker

Del Piero's glaring misses in the Euro 2000 final – which Italy lost to a Golden Goal – still haunt him, so the Juve ace has a chance to put that right. Like Francesco Totti, he gives the side more than goals – clever movement and dribbling make him a real handful, and if Del Piero hits top form, Italy will be flying!

CHRISTIAN VIERI ★ Striker

Vieri will go into Euro 2004 after a difficult domestic season that saw him linked with a move away from Inter Milan almost every week. Inter's signing of Adriano fuelled more gossip about his future, but Vieri is still Italy's No.1 centre-forward and will almost certainly be among the tournament's leading scorers.

★ WHO PLAYED IN ITALY'S EURO 2004 QUALIFYING GAMES? ★

AZERBAIJAN	SERBIA & MON	WALES	FINLAND	FINLAND	WALES	SERBIA & MON	AZERBAIJAN
Won 2-0 (a) *og	Drew 1-1 (h)	Lost 2-1 (a)	Won 2-0 (h)	Won 2-0 (a)	Won 4-0 (h)	Drew 1-1 (a)	Won 4-0 (h)
Buffon	Buffon	Buffon	Buffon	Buffon	Buffon	Buffon	Buffon
Panucci	Panucci	Panucci	Panucci	Panucci	Panucci	Panucci	Oddo
Coco	Zauri	Zauri	Zambrotta	Zambrotta	Zambrotta	Zambrotta	Zambrotta
Nesta	Nesta	Nesta	Nesta	Nesta	Nesta	Nesta	Nesta
Cannavaro	Cannavaro	Cannavaro	Cannavaro	Cannavaro	Cannavaro	Cannavaro	Cannavaro
Di Biagio	Pirlo	Di Biagio	Zanetti	Zanetti	Zanetti	Tacchinardi	Zanetti
Tommasi	Gattuso	Pirlo	Perrotta	Perrotta	Perrotta	Perrotta	Perrotta
Gattuso	Tommasi	Ambrosini	Camoranesi	Fiore	Camoranesi	Camoranesi	Camoranesi
Del Piero 1	Doni	Tommasi	Totti	Totti 1	Del Piero 1	Del Piero	Totti
Vieri	Del Piero 1	Del Piero 1	Vieri 2	Del Piero 1	Vieri	Vieri	Vieri 1
Inzaghi	Inzaghi	Montella	Delvecchio	Corradi	Inzaghi 3	Inzaghi 1	Inzaghi 2
Substitutes:	Substitutes:	Substitutes:	Substitutes:	Substitutes:	Substitutes:	Substitutes:	Substitutes:
Ambrosini 57	Montella 46	Gattuso 54	Birindelli 70	Oddo 82	Oddo 58	Gattuso 51	Di Vaio 53
Montella 58	Ambrosini 78	Maccarone 69	Corradi 82	Delvecchio 84	Gattuso 74	Fiore 64	Ferrari 76
Pirlo 76	Oddo 81	Marazzina 85	Miccoli 87	Legrottaglie 89	Fiore 85	Corradi 85	Gattuso 86

Alessandro Nesta.

MATCHMAN'S VERDICT!

"Ciao! These geezers look cool an' play even better! Totti, Del Piero, Vieri – da names sound wicked, innit? If they don't muff it up World Cup stylee, I is backing 'em to make da semis at least!"

GROUP C
- ITALY
- **SWEDEN**
- DENMARK
- BULGARIA

SWEDEN

★ THE QUALIFYING SQUAD ★

Goalkeepers

Eddie Gustafsson
Club: Molde
Age: 27 ★ Caps/Goals: 4/0

Magnus Hedman
Club: Celtic
Age: 31 ★ Caps/Goals: 54/0

Andreas Isaksson
Club: Djurgardens
Age: 22 ★ Caps/Goals: 16/0

Magnus Hedman.

Defenders

Michael Svensson.

Nils-Eric Johansson
Club: Blackburn
Age: 24 ★ Caps/Goals: 4/0

Tommy Jonsson
Club: Halmstads
Age: 28 ★ Caps/Goals: 3/0

Teddy Lucic
Club: Bayer Leverkusen
Age: 31 ★ Caps/Goals: 57/0

Mikael Dorsin
Club: Strasbourg
Age: 22 ★ Caps/Goals: 5/0

Olof Mellberg
Club: Aston Villa
Age: 26 ★ Caps/Goals: 40/1

Erik Edman
Club: Heerenveen
Age: 25 ★ Caps/Goals: 17/0

Johan Mjallby
Club: Celtic
Age: 33 ★ Caps/Goals: 44/4

Andreas Jakobsson
Club: Brondby
Age: 31 ★ Caps/Goals: 30/1

Michael Svensson
Club: Southampton
Age: 28 ★ Caps/Goals: 25/0

Midfielders

Niclas Alexandersson
Club: Gothenburg
Age: 32 ★ Caps/Goals: 68/7

Anders Andersson
Club: Benfica
Age: 30 ★ Caps/Goals: 20/2

Christoffer Andersson
Club: Helsingborgs
Age: 25 ★ Caps/Goals: 18/0

Pontus Farnerud
Club: Strasbourg
Age: 24 ★ Caps/Goals: 7/0

Andreas Johansson
Club: Djurgardens
Age: 25 ★ Caps/Goals: 11/0

Kim Kallstrom
Club: Rennes
Age: 21 ★ Caps/Goals: 15/1

Christoffer Andersson.

Tobias Linderoth
Club: Everton
Age: 25 ★ Caps/Goals: 32/1

Freddie Ljungberg
Club: Arsenal
Age: 27 ★ Caps/Goals: 39/3

Mikael Nilsson
Club: Halmstads
Age: 25 ★ Caps/Goals: 13/3

Anders Svensson
Club: Southampton
Age: 27 ★ Caps/Goals: 43/10

Magnus Svensson
Club: Halmstads
Age: 35 ★ Caps/Goals: 32/2

Anders Svensson.

Strikers

Marcus Allback
Club: Aston Villa
Age: 30 ★ Caps/Goals: 36/16

Andreas Andersson
Club: AIK Stockholm
Age: 30 ★ Caps/Goals: 42/8

Zlatan Ibrahimovic
Club: Ajax
Age: 22 ★ Caps/Goals: 19/6

Mattias Jonson
Club: FC Copenhagen
Age: 30 ★ Caps/Goals: 36/6

Rade Prica
Club: Hansa Rostock
Age: 23 ★ Caps/Goals: 6/0

Stefan Selakovic
Club: Heerenveen
Age: 27 ★ Caps/Goals: 10/4

Niklas Skoog
Club: Malmo
Age: 29 ★ Caps/Goals: 8/4

Mattias Jonson.

Latvia were the only team to beat Sweden in qualifying.

*Don't be too shocked if dark horses **SWEDEN** spring some surprise results at Euro 2004!*

HOW DID THEY QUALIFY?

Sweden won their group despite a sloppy start. They began with a goalless draw away to Latvia and then dropped points at home to Hungary. But Sweden won the next five games and really enjoyed themselves in the matches against San Marino and Poland, scoring 16 goals without conceding any. That secured qualification, and a good job too – Sweden lost their final match at home to Latvia. It was a rare defeat – Sweden's first in qualifying since 1997!

WHAT ARE SWEDEN'S STRENGTHS?

Strong in defence, they only conceded three goals in eight qualifying games. Young goalkeeper Andreas Isaksson made a sound start to international footy and was well protected by Olof Mellberg, Michael Svensson and Andreas Jakobsson. One thing's for sure – opposing teams will have to work hard to score against the Swedes!

AND THEIR WEAKNESSES?

Henrik Larsson's retirement from international football – though he made a brief return in qualifying against Hungary – has left a gap in attack. Zlatan Ibrahimovic gives the Swedes some class up front, and his most likely strike partner will be Aston Villa's Marcus Allback – Sweden's top scorer in qualifying for the tournament. But the pair will have a big job on their hands in Portugal – it's difficult to replace a legend like Larsson and he'll be missed at Euro 2004.

HOW WILL THEY DO?

Sweden will believe they can get something out of every match. Italy will no doubt be favourites to win Group C, but there isn't very much to choose between the Swedes, Denmark and Bulgaria. It could come down to the last game of the group – a battle of Scandinavia between Sweden and Denmark for the runners-up spot. If they reach the quarter-finals, they'll be happy.

Marcus Allback missed a penalty against Latvia.

★ SWEDEN'S STRONGEST LINE-UP ★

ISAKSSON

EDMAN — MELLBERG — M SVENSSON — LUCIC

NILSSON — KALLSTROM — A SVENSSON — LJUNGBERG

IBRAHIMOVIC — ALLBACK

★ FINAL QUALIFYING TABLE ★

TEAM	P	W	D	L	F	A	PTS
1. SWEDEN	8	5	2	1	19	3	17
2. LATVIA	8	5	1	2	10	6	16
3. POLAND	8	4	1	3	11	7	13
4. HUNGARY	8	3	2	3	15	9	11
5. SAN MARINO	8	0	0	8	0	30	0

Sweden won the group by a point from Latvia.

SWEDEN STATS & FACTS!

MANAGER: Lars Lagerback & Tommy Soderberg

CAPTAIN: Olof Mellberg

MOST CAPS (Current Squad): Niclas Alexandersson, 68

MOST GOALS (Qualifying): Marcus Allback, 5

WORLD RANKING: 19th

ODDS TO WIN EURO 2004: 26/1

PREVIOUS TOURNAMENTS

EURO 2000: Group Stages

BEST EVER: Semi-finals, 1992

★ SWEDEN'S STAR MEN ★

ANDREAS ISAKSSON ★ Goalkeeper

The youngster replaced Magnus Hedman after the first qualifying match against Latvia and kept his place from then on. Although he's only 22 years old, Isaksson has already tasted football's highs and lows – signed by Juventus as a teenager, he was then sold on to Djurgardens without playing a game.

OLOF MELLBERG ★ Defender

Mellberg was voted Sweden's Player Of The Year in 2003 – proof that he's a rising star for the national team. The 26-year-old began the qualifying campaign at right-back, but he's more likely to partner Michael Svensson or the versatile Andreas Jakobsson in central defence. Quick, brave and strong, not many strikers will get the better of Mellberg.

FREDDIE LJUNGBERG ★ Midfielder

In Ljungberg, Sweden have a match-winner and will hope he can avoid the kind of niggly injuries which ruined his World Cup in 2002. The Arsenal ace usually operates on the left of Sweden's midfield and is always trying to make his trademark runs into the opposition penalty box – where he creates utter chaos!

★ WHO PLAYED IN SWEDEN'S EURO 2004 QUALIFYING GAMES? ★

LATVIA	HUNGARY	HUNGARY	SAN MARINO	POLAND	SAN MARINO	POLAND	LATVIA
Drew 0-0 (a)	Drew 1-1 (h)	Won 2-1 (a)	Won 6-0 (a)	Won 3-0 (h)	Won 5-0 (h)	Won 2-0 (a)	Lost 1-0 (h)
Hedman	Isaksson	Isaksson	Isaksson	Isaksson	Isaksson	Isaksson	Isaksson
Mellberg	Mellberg	Edman	Edman	Edman	Edman	Edman	Mellberg
Antonelius	Antonelius	Lucic	Lucic	Lucic	Lucic	Lucic	Lucic
M Svensson	M Svensson	M Svensson	Jakobsson	Jakobsson	M Svensson	M Svensson	M Svensson
Jakobsson	Jakobsson	Mellberg	Mellberg	Mellberg	Mellberg	Mellberg 1	Mellberg
Linderoth	Linderoth	Mjallby	Mjallby	Mjallby	Jakobsson 1	Jakobsson	C Andersson
Alexandersson	Alexandersson	A Andersson	A Andersson	Nilsson	Nilsson	Nilsson 1	Nilsson
Farnerud	A Svensson	A Svensson	Kallstrom	A Svensson 2	A Svensson	A Svensson	A Svensson
Mag Svensson	Ljungberg	Ljungberg	Ljungberg 1	Ljungberg	Kallstrom 1	Ljungberg	Kallstrom
Allback	A Andersson	Allback 2	Allback 2	Allback 1	Ibrahimovic 2	Allback	Allback
Ibrahimovic	Ibrahimovic 1	Larsson	Jonson 3	Jonson	Jonson 1	Jonson	Jonson
Substitutes:	Substitutes:	Substitutes:	Substitutes:	Substitutes:	Substitutes:	Substitutes:	Substitutes:
Jonson 56	Kallstrom 59	Kallstrom 60	A Svensson 56	Mag. Svensson 71	Linderoth 65	A Andersson 85	Dorsin 46
Kallstrom 75	Jonson 67	Jonson 89	A Johansson 73	M Svensson 88	A Johansson 68	Ibrahimovic 88	Ibrahimovic 64
NE Johansson 79	Allback 77		Nilsson 73		Skoog 73		A Johansson 80

Zlatan Ibrahimovic.

MATCHMAN'S VERDICT!

"How will Sweden do without Henrik 'Da Legend' Larsson? Well, da coaches 'ad better figure it out fast coz gettin' goals could be da key to Sweden's tournament!"

DENMARK

Goalkeepers

Jimmy Nielsen
Club: Aalborg
Age: 26 ★ Caps/Goals: 0/0

Peter Skov-Jensen
Club: FC Midtjylland
Age: 33 ★ Caps/Goals: 2/0

Thomas Sorensen
Club: Aston Villa
Age: 28 ★ Caps/Goals: 32/0

Thomas Sorensen.

Defenders

Thomas Helveg.

Rene Henriksen
Club: Panathinaikos
Age: 34 ★ Caps/Goals: 58/0

Niclas Jensen
Club: Borussia Dortmund
Age: 29 ★ Caps/Goals: 26/0

Martin Laursen
Club: AC Milan
Age: 26 ★ Caps/Goals: 31/1

Martin Albrechtsen
Club: FC Copenhagen
Age: 24 ★ Caps/Goals: 3/0

Steven Lustu
Club: Lyn
Age: 33 ★ Caps/Goals: 7/0

Kasper Bogelund
Club: PSV Eindhoven
Age: 23 ★ Caps/Goals: 8/0

Per Nielsen
Club: Brondby
Age: 30 ★ Caps/Goals: 4/0

Thomas Helveg
Club: Inter Milan
Age: 32 ★ Caps/Goals: 81/2

Thomas Rytter
Club: Wolfsburg
Age: 30 ★ Caps/Goals: 4/0

Midfielders

Per Frandsen
Club: Bolton
Age: 34 ★ Caps/Goals: 23/0

Thomas Gravsesen
Club: Everton
Age: 28 ★ Caps/Goals: 42/5

Jesper Gronkjaer
Club: Chelsea
Age: 26 ★ Caps/Goals: 42/4

Claus Jensen
Club: Charlton
Age: 27 ★ Caps/Goals: 26/5

Martin Jorgensen
Club: Udinese
Age: 28 ★ Caps/Goals: 47/8

Jan Michaelsen
Club: Panathinaikos
Age: 33 ★ Caps/Goals: 19/1

Claus Jensen.

Christian Poulsen
Club: Schalke
Age: 24 ★ Caps/Goals: 16/0

Thomas Roll Larsen
Club: FC Copenhagen
Age: 27 ★ Caps/Goals: 7/1

Dennis Rommedahl
Club: PSV Eindhoven
Age: 25 ★ Caps/Goals: 38/9

Thomas Schultz
Club: Hansa Rostock
Age: 27 ★ Caps/Goals: 1/0

Morten Wieghorst
Club: Brondby
Age: 33 ★ Caps/Goals: 29/3

Martin Jorgensen.

Strikers

Soren Berg
Club: Odense
Age: 28 ★ Caps/Goals: 1/0

Morten Skoubo
Club: Borussia Monchengladbach
Age: 23 ★ Caps/Goals: 1/0

Kasper Dalgas
Club: Brondby
Age: 28 ★ Caps/Goals: 0/0

Jon Dahl Tomasson
Club: AC Milan
Age: 27 ★ Caps/Goals: 56/26

Peter Lovenkrands
Club: Glasgow Rangers
Age: 24 ★ Caps/Goals: 9/0

Peter Madsen
Club: VFL Bochum
Age: 26 ★ Caps/Goals: 7/0

Ebbe Sand
Club: Schalke 04
Age: 31 ★ Caps/Goals: 60/20

Ebbe Sand.

The Danes saw off Romania to finish as group winners.

Jon Dahl Tomasson is Denmark's deadly striker!

Euro '92 winners DENMARK have enough attacking flair to make an impact again!

HOW DID THEY QUALIFY?

The Danes deserve some praise for making it through ahead of Norway, Romania and a strong Bosnia-Herzegovina side. Drawing with Norway and then beating Luxembourg was easy, but a 5-2 win in Romania really kicked-off the campaign. A 2-0 home defeat to the Bosnians threatened to put the skids on, but Denmark went unbeaten in the final four matches to coast through to the finals.

WHAT ARE DENMARK'S STRENGTHS?

While the England squad would love to have just one winger with pace and directness, the Danes almost have too many of them! Peter Lovenkrands, Martin Jorgensen, Dennis Rommedahl and Chelsea's Jesper Gronkjaer are all quick, attacking players who can operate wide. In fact, Denmark coach Morten Olsen has a bit of a problem fitting them all in!

AND THEIR WEAKNESSES?

Denmark play an open, attacking game which is great when the team is on top, but it can blow up in their faces if they're not careful. With two flying wingers in the side, midfielders Claus Jensen and Thomas Gravesen have plenty of work to do when the pressure is on, and the team can get overrun. Jensen's strength is on the ball too, so Denmark's defence doesn't get a lot of cover at times!

HOW WILL THEY DO?

Can Denmark push on and challenge for the trophy? The team isn't among the favourites, but neither was the side which beat Germany in the final of Euro '92. They have the talent to win matches, and the Danes will gain belief from beating France in the last World Cup and England in last year's friendly. They could edge out Sweden to make the quarter-finals at least!

★ DENMARK'S STRONGEST LINE-UP ★

SORENSEN

HENRIKSEN — HELVEG — LAURSEN — N JENSEN

C JENSEN — GRAVESEN

ROMMEDAHL — GRONKJAER

JORGENSEN

TOMASSON

★ FINAL QUALIFYING TABLE ★

TEAM	P	W	D	L	F	A	PTS
1. DENMARK	8	4	3	1	15	9	15
2. NORWAY	8	4	2	2	9	5	14
3. ROMANIA	8	4	2	2	21	9	14
4. BOSNIA-HERZEGOVINA	8	4	1	3	7	8	13
5. LUXEMBOURG	8	0	0	8	0	21	0

Denmark only lost once in qualifying.

DENMARK STATS & FACTS!

MANAGER: Morten Olsen

CAPTAIN: Rene Henriksen

MOST CAPS (Current Squad):
Thomas Helveg, 81

MOST GOALS (Qualifying):
Jon-Dahl Tomasson, 5

WORLD RANKING: 13th

ODDS TO WIN EURO 2004: 28/1

PREVIOUS TOURNAMENTS

EURO 2000: Group Stages

BEST EVER: Winners, 1992

THOMAS GRAVESEN ★ Midfielder

Gravesen is well known to English footy fans because of his all-action Everton displays, but for Denmark, he's even more of a key figure. An ever-present during the qualifiers, the 28-year-old scored an incredible 45-yard lobbed goal in Romania, but his campaign ended with a red card against Bosnia.

DENNIS ROMMEDAHL ★ Midfielder

Rommedahl's scorching pace is no longer a big secret, but that doesn't mean he's any easier to stop! The PSV star's best position is on the right wing, where he's able to take on defenders, whip in crosses and score goals. He netted against France in World Cup 2002 and Denmark will expect him to be a major attacking threat once again.

JON DAHL TOMASSON ★ Striker

Tomasson's been in and out of the Milan line-up since signing from Feyenoord, but he's kept up his excellent international form with an impressive ratio of almost a goal every two games. After scoring four times in the last World Cup, he could be a leading contender for the Golden Boot at Euro 2004.

★ WHO PLAYED IN DENMARK'S EURO 2004 QUALIFYING GAMES? ★

NORWAY	LUXEMBOURG	ROMANIA	B-HERZEGOVINA	NORWAY	LUXEMBOURG	ROMANIA	B-HERZEGOVINA
Drew 2-2 (a)	*Won 2-0 (h)*	*Won 5-2 (a) *og*	*Lost 2-0 (h)*	*Won 1-0 (h)*	*Won 2-0 (a)*	*Drew 2-2 (h)*	*Drew 1-1 (a)*
Sorensen	Skov-Jensen	Sorensen	Sorensen	Sorensen	Sorensen	Sorensen	Sorensen
Lustu	Henriksen	Henriksen	Henriksen	Henriksen	Henriksen	Henriksen	Henriksen
N Jensen	N Jensen	N Jensen	N Jensen	N Jensen	N Jensen	N Jensen	N Jensen
Laursen	Bogelund	Laursen	Albrechtsen	Laursen	Laursen	Laursen 1	Laursen
Helveg	Poulsen	Rytter	Michaelsen	Helveg	Bogelund	Helveg	Helveg
Poulsen	C Jensen	Poulsen	C Jensen	Wieghorst	Wieghorst	Wieghorst	Wieghorst
Gravesen	Gravesen	Gravesen 1	Gravesen	Gravesen	Gravesen 1	Gravesen	Gravesen
Gronkjaer	Rommedahl	Lovenkrands	Rommedahl	Gronkjaer 1	Gronkjaer	Jorgensen	Poulsen
Rommedahl	Jorgensen	Rommedahl 2	Jorgensen	C Jensen	C Jensen 1	Gronkjaer	Jorgensen 1
Tomasson 2	Tomasson 1	Tomasson 1	Tomasson	Jorgensen	Jorgensen	Tomasson 1	Tomasson
Sand	Sand 1	Sand	Sand	Sand	Sand	Sand	Tomasson
Substitutes:	*Substitutes:*	*Substitutes:*	*Substitutes:*	*Substitutes:*	*Substitutes:*	*Substitutes:*	*Substitutes:*
C Jensen 70	Roll Larsen 67	Michaelsen 34	Wieghorst 58	Roll Larsen 62	Roll Larsen 51	C Jensen 54	Rommedahl 55
P Nielsen 89	Lovenkrands 75	Jorgensen 46	Frandsen 80	Rommedahl 69	Rommedahl 63	Poulsen 64	Roll Larsen 85
Michaelsen 89		Wieghorst 68	Berg 84	P Nielsen 82	Skoubo 74	Rommedahl 81	

Jesper Gronkjaer.

MATCHMAN'S VERDICT!

"Listen up Danish dudes! I is lovin' yer team coz it's full o' flyin' wingers! England duffed 'em up in da last World Cup but I recks Denmark will be one of da best Euro teams to watch!"

BULGARIA

★ THE QUALIFYING SQUAD ★

Goalkeepers

Dimitar Ivankov
Club: Levski Sofia
Age: 28 ★ **Caps/Goals:** 21/0

Stoyan Kolev
Club: CSKA Sofia
Age: 28 ★ **Caps/Goals:** 4/0

Zdravko Zdravkov
Club: Litex Lovech
Age: 33 ★ **Caps/Goals:** 60/0

Zdravko Zdravkov.

Defenders

Predrag Pazin.

Ivailo Petkov
Club: Fenerbahce
Age: 28 ★ **Caps/Goals:** 49/3

Georgi Petrov
Club: Taishan
Age: 30 ★ **Caps/Goals:** 6/0

Martin Stankov
Club: Levski Sofia
Age: 30 ★ **Caps/Goals:** 3/0

Ilian Stoianov
Club: Levski Sofia
Age: 27 ★ **Caps/Goals:** 19/0

Rosen Kirilov
Club: Litex Lovech
Age: 31 ★ **Caps/Goals:** 41/0

Elin Topuzakov
Club: Levski Sofia
Age: 27 ★ **Caps/Goals:** 7/0

Nikolai Krastev
Club: Naftex Bourgas
Age: 24 ★ **Caps/Goals:** 6/0

Zlatomir Zagoric
Club: Litex Lovech
Age: 32 ★ **Caps/Goals:** 19/0

Predrag Pazin
Club: Shakhtar Donetsk
Age: 31 ★ **Caps/Goals:** 27/0

Zhivko Zhelev
Club: Litex Lovech
Age: 24 ★ **Caps/Goals:** 4/0

Midfielders

Daniel Borimov
Club: Levski Sofia
Age: 34 ★ **Caps/Goals:** 64/5

Stilian Petrov
Club: Celtic
Age: 24 ★ **Caps/Goals:** 45/6

Velizar Dimitrov
Club: CSKA Sofia
Age: 25 ★ **Caps/Goals:** 9/2

Todor Yanchev
Club: CSKA Sofia
Age: 28 ★ **Caps/Goals:** 16/0

Emil Gargorov
Club: CSKA Sofia
Age: 23 ★ **Caps/Goals:** 1/0

Marian Hristov
Club: Kaiserslautern
Age: 29 ★ **Caps/Goals:** 35/4

Martin Kamburov
Club: Lokomotiv Plovdiv
Age: 23 ★ **Caps/Goals:** 2/0

Georgi Peev
Club: Dynamo Kiev
Age: 25 ★ **Caps/Goals:** 36/0

Milen Petkov
Club: AEK Athens
Age: 30 ★ **Caps/Goals:** 36/0

Martin Kamburov.

Strikers

Dimitar Berbatov
Club: Bayer Leverkusen
Age: 23 ★ **Caps/Goals:** 27/15

Stokyo Sakaliev
Club: CSKA Sofia
Age: 25 ★ **Caps/Goals:** 2/0

Georgi Chilikov
Club: Levski Sofia
Age: 25 ★ **Caps/Goals:** 5/1

Svetoslav Todorov
Club: Portsmouth
Age: 25 ★ **Caps/Goals:** 32/4

Zoran Jankovic
Club: Litex Lovech
Age: 30 ★ **Caps/Go**

Zdravko Lazarov
Club: Gaziantepspor
Age: 28 ★ **Caps/Goals:** 3/0

Vladimir Manchev
Club: Lille
Age: 26 ★ **Caps/Goals:** 12/1

Martin Petrov
Club: Wolfsburg
Age: 25 ★ **Caps/Goals:** 37/4

Zoran Jankovic.

Can Bulgaria spring a few surprises at Euro 2004?

Dimitar Berbatov is Bulgaria's main goalscoring threat.

After six years out in the cold, Euro 2004 is the start of a new era for **BULGARIA**!

HOW DID THEY QUALIFY?

Bulgaria got through with five wins, two draws and just one loss, and the defeat came when it didn't matter – as Bulgaria had already won the group! But the campaign had problems – captain Krassimir Balakov was due to retire at the end of qualifying but he quit early, then Charlton's Radostin Kishishev packed it in after he wasn't named as the new skipper!

WHAT ARE BULGARIA'S STRENGTHS?

It's a young squad with a good team spirit – and that's raised confidence ahead of Euro 2004. Apparently, the squad relaxes before matches by going to the cinema together – and even Bulgaria's most famous player, Hristo Stoichkov, has been impressed with the current crop. Stilian Petrov and Georgi Peev are the creative talents in midfield, and forwards Dimitar Berbatov, Martin Petrov and Vladimir Manchev are all capable goalscorers.

AND THEIR WEAKNESSES?

Bulgaria are a team that's being re-built, and although everything is going well, this tournament may have come a bit too soon for them. Losing Balakov and Kishishev was a blow, because their experience would have been valuable – and losing the Charlton right-back in particular has left Bulgaria's defence under-strength. Coach Plamen Markov still hasn't decided who his best replacement is.

HOW WILL THEY DO?

Bulgaria will go into this tournament as outsiders to progress from Group C. The best is yet to come from Bulgaria, and after missing out on the last World Cup as well as Euro 2000, the team will just want to play well again in a major tournament. But with Berbatov, Manchev and the two Petrovs in the side, the Bulgarians could still spring the odd surprise result this summer!

★ BULGARIA'S STRONGEST LINE-UP ★

ZDRAVKOV

STANKOV — KIRILOV — PAZIN — I PETKOV

PEEV — S PETROV — HRISTOV

M PETROV — BERBATOV — MANCHEV

★ FINAL QUALIFYING TABLE ★

TEAM	P	W	D	L	F	A	PTS
1. BULGARIA	8	5	2	1	13	4	17
2. CROATIA	8	5	1	2	12	4	16
3. BELGIUM	8	5	1	2	11	9	16
4. ESTONIA	8	2	2	4	4	6	8
5. ANDORRA	8	0	0	8	1	18	0

Bulgaria topped their qualifying group.

BULGARIA STATS & FACTS!

MANAGER: Plamen Markov	**WORLD RANKING:** 34th
CAPTAIN: Stilian Petrov	**ODDS TO WIN EURO 2004:** 50/1
MOST CAPS (Current Squad): Daniel Borimov, 64	**PREVIOUS TOURNAMENTS**
MOST GOALS (Qualifying): Dimitar Berbatov, 5	**EURO 2000:** Did Not Qualify
	BEST EVER: Quarter-finals, 1968

★ BULGARIA'S STAR MEN ★

STILIAN PETROV ★ Midfielder

Petrov is Bulgaria's best player – and that's official! Stilian was voted Bulgarian Player Of The Year in 2003 and is the team's brightest talent. Captain of the national side at just 24 years old, the classy Celtic star will be the playmaker in the Bulgarian midfield and will be hoping to score a goal or two himself!

MARTIN PETROV ★ Striker

Petrov's international career has come a long way since he was sent off against England in 1999. He was breaking into Bulgaria's line-up then, but now he's one of the team's key men. The quick winger was linked with a move to Barcelona a couple of years ago, but stayed in the Bundesliga with Wolfsburg instead.

VLADIMIR MANCHEV ★ Striker

Manchev didn't play a huge part in Bulgaria's qualifying success but his impressive club form can't be ignored. The 26-year-old spent 2003-04 scoring loads for French side Lille, boasting a better ratio than a goal every two games! He also strengthened his case for a starting place with the winner over South Korea during the build-up to Euro 2004.

★ WHO PLAYED IN BULGARIA'S EURO 2004 QUALIFYING GAMES? ★

BELGIUM		CROATIA		ANDORRA		ESTONIA		BELGIUM		ESTONIA		ANDORRA		CROATIA	
Won 2-0 (a)		Won 2-0 (h)		Won 2-1 (h)		Drew 0-0 (a)		Drew 2-2 (h)		Won 2-0 (h)		Won 3-0 (a)		Lost 1-0 (a)	
Zdravkov		Zdravkov		Zdravkov		Zdravkov		Zdravkov		Ivankov		Ivankov		Zdravkov	
Kishishev		Kishishev		Kishishev		Kishishev		Stankov		Borimov		Borimov		Krastev	
I Petkov		I Petkov		I Petkov		I Petkov		I Petkov		I Petkov		I Petkov		I Petkov	
Kirilov		Kirilov		Kirilov		Kirilov		Kirilov		Kirilov		Kirilov		Kirilov	
Pazin		Pazin		Pazin		Pazin		Stoianov		Stoianov		Pazin		Pazin	
Balakov		Balakov		Balakov 1		Balakov		Borimov		Borimov		Hristov 1		Borimov	
Peev		Peev		Peev		Peev		Hristov		Dimitrov		Peev		Dimitrov	
Stilian Petrov 1		Stilian Petrov 1		Stilian Petrov		Stilian Petrov		Dimitrov		Stilian Petrov		Stilian Petrov		Peev	
M Petrov		Jankovic		M Petrov		M Petrov		Stilian Petrov		M Petrov 1		M Petrov		Hristov	
M Petrov		M Petrov		Jankovic		Berbatov		M Petrov		Berbatov 1		Jankovic		Stilian Petrov	
Jankovic 1		Berbatov 1		Chilikov 1		Jankovic		Berbatov 1		Jankovic		Berbatov 2		Berbatov	
Substitutes:		*Substitutes:*		*Substitutes:*		*Substitutes:*		*Substitutes:*		*Substitutes:*		*Substitutes:*		*Substitutes:*	
G Petrov	83	Chilikov	39	Svetoslav Petrov	61	Todorov	46	Krastev	53	Krastev	63	Dimitrov	58	Manchev	63
Zagoric	89	G Petrov	66	Manchev	75	M Petkov	70	Todorov 1	60	Peev	72	Manchev	63	Jankovic	72
				Gonzo	77			Alexandrov	72	Zhelev	88				

Ivailo Petkov.

MATCHMAN'S VERDICT!

"Me Celtic buddy Stilian Petrov is Bulgaria's skipper and 'e recks they ain't there to make up da numbers! These boyz won't just roll over, anywayz!"

NAFF NAMES!
Croatia Star
Jerko Leko

GOOD JOB I WASN'T CALLED LEGO!

FIFA WORLD RANKINGS!

So just how good are the teams at Euro 2004? Find out here!

FRANCE	2nd
SPAIN	3rd
HOLLAND	4th
CZECH REPUBLIC	6th
ENGLAND	9th
ITALY	10th
GERMANY	12th
DENMARK	13th
PORTUGAL	17th
SWEDEN	19th
CROATIA	20th
RUSSIA	24th
GREECE	30th
BULGARIA	34th
SWITZERLAND	44th
LATVIA	53rd

DR. FOOTY'S EURO PLAYER

1 When you're watching a game of footy, you most like to see...

- **A** Super-tough tackles and long-range shots! — **1** point
- **B** Plenty of tricks and flashy passing! — **3** points
- **C** Goals, goals and even more goals! — **5** points
- **D** Passion and spirit from all your team-mates! — **7** points

2 All your team-mates know that you're the type of player who...

- **A** Will work your socks off for the whole game! — **1** point
- **B** Can change the game in a split second! — **3** points
- **C** Is almost certain to score a goal in every match! — **5** points
- **D** Can motivate them when the going gets tough! — **7** points

3 You have lots of good things in your game, but you must learn how to...

- **A** Keep your long-range shots on target! — **1** point
- **B** Not embarrass the opposition too much! — **3** points
- **C** Stay onside a bit more! — **5** points
- **D** Use your left foot sometimes! — **7** points

4 You love playing in lots of different positions, but your favourite is...

- **A** Just in front of the back four! — **1** point
- **B** A free role in midfield! — **3** points
- **C** Up front all on your own! — **5** points
- **D** Slap-bang in the centre of midfield! — **7** points

5 In the Euro Championships final, you'd like your team to play...

- **A** England, because you usually beat them! — **1** point
- **B** Anyone, because you'll win anyway! — **3** points
- **C** Better than they did in the qualifiers! — **5** points
- **D** Germany, coz you owe them for Euro '96! — **7** points

6 Your favourite team should win the Euro 2004 trophy because...

- **A** They just missed out on the last World Cup! — **1** point
- **B** They've got all the best players! — **3** points
- **C** They play the most attractive football! — **5** points
- **D** It's about time they won a trophy at last! — **7** points

MICHEL PLATINI
FRANCE, 1984

RUUD GULLIT
HOLLAND, 1988

LARS OLSEN
DENMARK, 1992

JURGEN KLINSMANN
GERMANY, 1996

DIDIER DESCHAMPS
FRANCE, 2000

TEST!

I'VE WORKED WITH EUROPE'S TOP PLAYERS AND THEY'VE ALL TAKEN MY PLAYER TEST! SO NOW YOU CAN HAVE A GO – TO SEE WHICH EURO 2004 STAR YOU ARE MOST LIKE!

YOUR SCORE:

6-14
You're most like... Dietmar Hamann!
You love the rough and tumble of a match, and you're happy to do all the hard work and let your team-mates take the headlines. You might not be the most exciting player, but the lads really struggle when you're not playing!

15-23
You're most like... Zinedine Zidane!
You've got more tricks than a wizard's sleeve! You know you're the most skilful player on the pitch, and you can be unstoppable on your day. You don't do much tackling these days, but then why the heck should you with all your skill?

24-32
You're most like... Ruud van Nistelrooy!
You're a goal machine! You don't really care about tactics or formations – all you want to do is get out on the pitch and stick the ball in the net. You get caught offside a lot, but that doesn't really bother you – as long as you're scoring goals!

33-42
You're most like... David Beckham!
You can pass, you can finish and you always give 100 per cent. Although you're not very loud, you make a good captain because you lead by example. You could use your left foot more – but with a right foot like yours, why bother?

THE EURO STAR!

Picking the best player at Euro 2004 is just too difficult, so MATCH has decided to mix 'em all together! This is what we reckon the ultimate Euro star would look like! Check out our choices, then write down who you'd pick instead!

RIGHT ARM
GIGI BUFFON
The most expensive goalkeeper ever is a cert for our perfect Euro star. It takes something special to get past Italy's big Buffon!

I'D PICK

BRAIN
LUIS FIGO
The Portugal ace can pass, dribble and finish – which makes him the perfect choice as the brain for our ultimate player!

I'D PICK

LEFT ARM
IKER CASILLAS
One of the best shot-stoppers in the world completes the other half of our unbeatable 'keeper. The Real Madrid guy's ace!

I'D PICK

RIGHT LEG
THIERRY HENRY
When you think of a player with electric pace and deadly finishing, then two words spring to mind – Thierry Henry. Fantastique!

I'D PICK

LEFT LEG
RAUL
We almost plumped for Italy's Christian Vieri here, but Raul's creativity just clinched it. The Spanish superstar is a legend!

I'D PICK

BODY
EDGAR DAVIDS!
If you're gonna be the best, you need a good engine – and no-one's got a better engine than Edgar 'The Pitbull' Davids!

I'D PICK

LE PREMIERSHIP!

France may be one of the hot favourites to win the European Championships this summer, but it's all thanks to the good old Premiership! What are we banging on about? Well, loads of French stars are regulars in the Prem, meaning France boss Jacques Santini could pick a team using only English-based players if he really wanted to!

BARTHEZ
MAN. UNITED

GALLAS
CHELSEA

DESAILLY
CHELSEA

SILVESTRE
MAN. UNITED

PIRES
ARSENAL

MAKELELE
CHELSEA

VIEIRA
ARSENAL

ROBERT
NEWCASTLE

WILTORD
ARSENAL

HENRY
ARSENAL

ANELKA
MAN. CITY

CZECH REPUBLIC

★ THE QUALIFYING SQUAD ★

Goalkeepers

Jaromir Blazek
Club: Sparta Prague
Age: 31 ★ Caps/Goals: 2/0

Petr Cech
Club: Rennes
Age: 21 ★ Caps/Goals: 15/0

Antonin Kinsky
Club: Saturn Ramenskoje
Age: 29 ★ Caps/Goals: 4/0

Petr Cech.

Defenders

Tomas Ujfalusi.

Tomas Hubschman
Club: Sparta Prague
Age: 22 ★ Caps/Goals: 13/0

Marek Jankulovski
Club: Udinese
Age: 27 ★ Caps/Goals: 25/6

Martin Jiranek
Club: Reggina
Age: 25 ★ Caps/Goals: 7/0

Petr Johana
Club: Sparta Prague
Age: 27 ★ Caps/Goals: 13/0

Rene Bolf
Club: Banik Ostrava
Age: 30 ★ Caps/Goals: 17/0

Adam Petrous
Club: Rubin Kaza
Age: 26 ★ Caps/Goals: 4/0

Zdenik Grygera
Club: Ajax
Age: 25 ★ Caps/Goals: 19/1

Tomas Ujfalusi
Club: Hamburg
Age: 26 ★ Caps/Goals: 26/2

Midfielders

Richard Dostalek
Club: Rubin Kaza
Age: 30 ★ Caps/Goals: 5/0

Tomas Galasek
Club: Ajax
Age: 31 ★ Caps/Goals: 29/0

Jiri Jarosik
Club: CSKA Moscow
Age: 26 ★ Caps/Goals: 18/0

Pavel Nedved
Club: Juventus
Age: 31 ★ Caps/Goals: 75/17

Karol Poborsky
Club: Sparta Prague
Age: 32 ★ Caps/Goals: 91/7

Roman Tyce.

Tomas Rosicky
Club: Borussia Dortmund
Age: 23 ★ Caps/Goals: 32/7

Vladimir Smicer
Club: Liverpool
Age: 31 ★ Caps/Goals: 66/24

Roman Tyce
Club: 1860 Munich
Age: 27 ★ Caps/Goals: 17/1

Stepan Vachousek
Club: Marseille
Age: 24 ★ Caps/Goals: 11/2

Petr Vorisek
Club: Sparta Prague
Age: 25 ★ Caps/Goals: 3/0

Tomas Rosicky.

Strikers

Milan Baros
Club: Liverpool
Age: 22 ★ Caps/Goals: 21/12

Marek Heinz
Club: Banik Ostrava
Age: 26 ★ Caps/Goals: 5/1

Jan Koller
Club: Borussia Dortmund
Age: 31 ★ Caps/Goals: 47/27

Vratislav Lokvenc
Club: Kaiserslautern
Age: 30 ★ Caps/Goals: 56/8

Jiri Stajner
Club: Sparta Prague
Age: 28 ★ Caps/Goals: 13/2

Milan Baros.

The Euro '96 runners-up have some top players.

Group D looks tough, but the Czechs have a strong team!

The CZECH REPUBLIC qualified easily and really fancy their chances at Euro 2004!

HOW DID THEY QUALIFY?

The Czech Republic's big threat in qualifying was Holland. But they saw off that challenge with seven wins and a draw – dropping just two points after a 1-1 draw with the Dutch in Rotterdam. Sticking 19 goals past Moldova, Belarus and Austria was impressive, and the 3-1 home win over Holland in September sealed top spot in their group and a place in Portugal!

WHAT ARE THE CZECH REPUBLIC'S STRENGTHS?

Their midfield. Pavel Nedved is one of the world's best attacking midfielders and with Karol Poborsky on the right, those two pose a big threat. Dortmund's Tomas Rosicky shines in central midfield or behind the striker, and Liverpool's Vladimir Smicer can play right across the middle. This team has a midfield that's packed with goals, vision and versatility!

AND THEIR WEAKNESSES?

Coach Karel Bruckner doesn't have a big squad, so if key players like Nedved and Poborsky are missing, he'll struggle for quality reserves. The Czech boss prefers players who have moved abroad to teams in the stronger European leagues, so Jiri Jarosik, Adam Petrous and Antonin Kinsky – who all play in Russia – are usually overlooked. The defence is also inexperienced at this level, which could be their biggest problem.

HOW WILL THEY DO?

The Czechs were a team of unknowns at Euro '96, but they reached the final and only lost to a Golden Goal. At Euro 2000 they were tipped by many to win it, but failed to even get out of their group! The Czech Republic must learn how to deal with the pressure, but if they get the right balance in a tough-looking Group D, they could go all the way – because they certainly have the talent!

★ CZECH REPUBLIC'S STRONGEST LINE-UP ★

CECH

GRYGERA — BOLF — UJFALUSI — JANKULOVSKI

GALASEK

POBORSKY — ROSICKY — NEDVED — SMICER

KOLLER

★ FINAL QUALIFYING TABLE ★

TEAM	P	W	D	L	F	A	PTS
1. CZECH REPUBLIC	8	7	1	0	23	5	22
2. HOLLAND	8	6	1	1	20	6	19
3. AUSTRIA	8	3	0	5	12	14	9
4. MOLDOVA	8	2	0	6	5	19	6
5. BELARUS	8	1	0	7	4	20	3

The Czechs pipped Holland to top spot.

CZECH REPUBLIC STATS & FACTS!

MANAGER: Karel Bruckner

CAPTAIN: Pavel Nedved

MOST CAPS (Current Squad):
Karol Poborsky, 91

MOST GOALS (Qualifying):
Jan Koller, 6

WORLD RANKING: 6th

ODDS TO WIN EURO 2004: 13/1

PREVIOUS TOURNAMENTS

EURO 2000: Group Stages

BEST EVER: Runners-up, 1996

★ CZECH REPUBLIC'S STAR MEN ★

KAROL POBORSKY ★ Midfielder

Even at 32, Poborsky is still a class act and one of his country's most important players. The former Manchester United and Lazio winger is a big threat down the right, and what he's lost in pace he makes up for with clever passing and powerful shooting. His experience will be important in Portugal.

PAVEL NEDVED ★ Midfielder

The 2003 European Footballer Of The Year goes into Euro 2004 in the best form of his career. Nedved usually starts on the left for the Czechs and then drifts all over the pitch, supporting the strikers and scaring the pants off defenders. He's a big-game player with a big reputation and he'll need to be watched!

JAN KOLLER ★ Striker

The Czech Republic's big striker might not look like a world-class player, but don't be fooled. He's very effective at what he does – holding up the ball, flicking on headers and powering past defenders. For a big man he's got good feet as well, and an international goalscoring record that compares with the very best. Koller could cause real problems!

★ WHO PLAYED IN THE CZECH REPUBLIC'S EURO 2004 QUALIFYING GAMES? ★

MOLDOVA		BELARUS		HOLLAND		AUSTRIA		MOLDOVA		BELARUS		HOLLAND		AUSTRIA	
Won 2-0 (a)		Won 2-0 (h)		Drew 1-1 (a)		Won 4-0 (h)		Won 5-0 (h)		Won 3-1 (a)		Won 3-1 (h)		Won 3-2 (a)	
Cech		Cech		Cech		Cech		Cech		Cech		Cech		Petrous	
Grygera		Jiranek		Grygera		Grygera		Grygera		Grygera		Grygera		Jankulovski	1
Jankulovski	1	Jankulovski		Jankulovski		Jankulovski	1	Jankulovski		Jankulovski		Jiranek		Bolf	
Bolf		Bolf		Bolf		Bolf		Bolf		Bolf		Bolf		Jiranek	
Ujfalusi		Ujfalusi		Ujfalusi		Ujfalusi		Ujfalusi		Ujfalusi		Ujfalusi		Galasek	
Galasek		Galasek		Galasek		Galasek		Galasek		Tyce		Galasek		Heinz	
Poborsky		Poborsky	1	Poborsky		Poborsky		Poborsky		Poborsky		Poborsky	1	Vachousek	1
Rosicky	1	Rosicky		Smicer		Smicer		Smicer	1	Rosicky		Smicer		Nedved	
Vachousek		Nedved		Nedved		Nedved	1	Nedved		Nedved	1	Nedved		Stajner	
Stajner		Baros	1	Rosicky		Baros		Rosicky		Baros	1	Rosicky		Lokvenc	
Koller		Koller		Koller	1	Koller	2	Koller	1	Koller		Koller	1		
Substitutes:		Substitutes:		Substitutes:		Substitutes:		Substitutes:		Substitutes:		Substitutes:		Substitutes:	
Jarovski	56	Vachousek	56	Jiranek	79	Rosicky	63	Baros	59	Smicer	1	35	Hubschman	25	Tyce	41
Lokvenc	84	Grygera	86	Lokvenc	88	Vachousek	74	Stajner	1	65	Hubschman	66	Baros	1	61	Koller	1	68
Dostalek	89	Jarosik	90			Lokvenc	88	Lokvenc	2	79	Vachousek	83	Vachousek	81	Vorisek	83

Tomas Hubschman.

MATCHMAN'S VERDICT!

"Czech out these dudes at Euro 2004! Ha, ha, ha! Soz for da naff joke, but dis team 'ave loadsa top players like Nedved an' Baros, innit! They could go far if they 'ave a wicked start!"

GERMANY

Germany are hoping to repeat their 2002 World Cup form.

Will Fredi Bobic and Germany have much to shout about at Euro 2004?

★ THE QUALIFYING SQUAD ★

Goalkeepers

Oliver Kahn
Club: Bayern Munich
Age: 34 ★ Caps/Goals: 66/0

Jens Lehmann
Club: Arsenal
Age: 34 ★ Caps/Goals: 16/0

Frank Rost
Club: Schalke
Age: 30 ★ Caps/Goals: 4/0

Jens Lehmann.

Defenders

Frank Baumann.

Phillip Lahm
Club: Stuttgart
Age: 20 ★ Caps/Goals: 1/0

Christophe Metzelder
Club: Borussia Dortmund
Age: 23 ★ Caps/Goals: 16/0

Jens Nowotny
Club: Bayer Leverkusen
Age: 30 ★ Caps/Goals: 39/0

Christian Rahn
Club: Hamburg
Age: 24 ★ Caps/Goals: 4/0

Frank Baumann
Club: Werder Bremen
Age: 28 ★ Caps/Goals: 22/2

Tobias Rau
Club: Bayern Munich
Age: 22 ★ Caps/Goals: 7/1

Arne Friedrich
Club: Hertha Berlin
Age: 24 ★ Caps/Goals: 15/0

Marko Rehmer
Club: Hertha Berlin
Age: 32 ★ Caps/Goals: 34/4

Andreas Hinkel
Club: Stuttgart
Age: 22 ★ Caps/Goals: 5/0

Christian Worns
Club: Borussia Dortmund
Age: 32 ★ Caps/Goals: 53/0

Midfielders

Michael Ballack
Club: Bayern Munich
Age: 27 ★ Caps/Goals: 37/14

Fabian Ernst
Club: Werder Bremen
Age: 25 ★ Caps/Goals: 3/0

Daniel Bierofka
Club: Bayer Leverkusen
Age: 25 ★ Caps/Goals: 3/1

Paul Freier
Club: Bochum
Age: 24 ★ Caps/Goals: 14/1

Jorge Bohme
Club: Schalke
Age: 30 ★ Caps/Goals: 10/1

Torsten Frings
Club: Borussia Dortmund
Age: 27 ★ Caps/Goals: 24/2

Sebastian Deisler
Club: Bayern Munich
Age: 24 ★ Caps/Goals: 20/3

Dietmar Hamann
Club: Liverpool
Age: 30 ★ Caps/Goals: 50/4

Jens Jeremies
Club: Bayern Munich
Age: 30 ★ Caps/Goals: 50/1

Sebastian Kehl
Club: Borussia Dortmund
Age: 24 ★ Caps/Goals: 21/3

Carsten Ramelow
Club: Bayer Leverkusen
Age: 30 ★ Caps/Goals: 45/3

Bernd Schneider
Club: Bayer Leverkusen
Age: 30 ★ Caps/Goals: 32/1

Jens Jeremies.

Strikers

Fredi Bobic
Club: Hertha Berlin
Age: 32 ★ Caps/Goals: 31/9

Oliver Neuville
Club: Bayer Leverkusen
Age: 31 ★ Caps/Goals: 46/4

Carsten Jancker
Club: Udinese
Age: 29 ★ Caps/Goals: 33/10

Miroslav Klose
Club: Kaiserslautern
Age: 25 ★ Caps/Goals: 35/15

Kevin Kuranyi
Club: Stuttgart
Age: 22 ★ Caps/Goals: 8/1

Benjamin Lauth
Club: 1860 Munich
Age: 22 ★ Caps/Goals: 4/0

Miroslav Klose.

World Cup 2002 runners-up GERMANY could find the going tough in the 'Group Of Death'!

HOW DID THEY QUALIFY?

It wasn't all plain sailing for the three-times European champions, despite being drawn in one of the easier groups. Things started with wins over Lithuania and the Faroe Islands, but draws in the return with Lithuania and Scotland meant the Scots and Iceland were back in it. A 2-1 win against Scotland put them back in the driving seat, before a 3-0 victory over Iceland sealed their place at Euro 2004.

WHAT ARE GERMANY'S STRENGTHS?

Rudi Voller has a side that can change formation depending on the opposition and the players available. For most of the qualifiers he's started with 3-5-2, switching to 4-4-2 if needed. Whatever system the Germans play, it's used to get the best out of their one world-class player – Michael Ballack – who is without doubt the key to their success.

AND THEIR WEAKNESSES?

Question marks remain over their attack. Young Stuttgart striker Kevin Kuranyi had a decent season and should start up front with Miroslav Klose, but this pairing won't strike fear into their Group D rivals. Carsten Jancker has had a poor season with Udinese and is well down Voller's pecking order, while 32-year-old Fredi Bobic was dropped from the Hertha Berlin side this season with doubts over his attitude.

HOW WILL THEY DO?

That's a tough one. While Germany had their critics in qualifying, they still finished unbeaten in their group. These days they almost seem to enjoy not being favourites for major tournaments and that spurs them on – just like at the 2002 World Cup. They could go all the way again this summer, or they could go out in the first round!

★ GERMANY'S STRONGEST LINE-UP ★

KAHN

FRIEDRICH   WORNS   BAUMANN   RAU

FRINGS   BALLACK   HAMANN   JEREMIES

KLOSE   KURANYI

★ FINAL QUALIFYING TABLE ★

TEAM	P	W	D	L	F	A	PTS
1. GERMANY	8	5	3	0	13	4	18
2. SCOTLAND	8	4	2	2	12	8	14
3. ICELAND	8	4	1	3	11	9	13
4. LITHUANIA	8	3	1	4	7	11	10
5. FAROE ISLANDS	8	0	1	7	7	18	1

Ballack and co. topped their qualifying group.

GERMANY STATS & FACTS!

MANAGER: Rudi Voller

CAPTAIN: Oliver Kahn

MOST CAPS (Current Squad): Oliver Kahn, 66

MOST GOALS (Qualifying): Michael Ballack & Fredi Bobic, 4

WORLD RANKING: 12th

ODDS TO WIN EURO 2004: 19/1

PREVIOUS TOURNAMENTS

EURO 2000: Group Stages

BEST EVER: Winners, 1972, 1980, 1996

★ GERMANY'S STAR MEN ★

OLIVER KAHN ★ Goalkeeper

Voted FIFA's best player at the 2002 World Cup, monster 'keeper Oliver Kahn is still one of the best in the world – even at the age of 34! With superb reflexes, surprising agility and a scary authority over his defenders, the Bayern Munich legend will hope to skipper Germany to glory in Portugal.

CHRISTIAN WORNS ★ Defender

With his Borussia Dortmund team-mate Christoph Metzelder struggling to regain full fitness, the experienced Worns could be his country's key man at the back at Euro 2004. Whether playing in a back three or four, his cool, calm head will be vital alongside youngsters like Tobias Rau and Christian Rahn in Germany's defence.

MICHAEL BALLACK ★ Midfielder

Germany coach Rudi Voller would like to wrap his star midfielder in cotton wool until the finals in Portugal – that's how important Ballack is to the national team! With four goals in the qualifying stages, the Bayern Munich star pulls the strings in midfield and has really grown into his playmaker role.

★ WHO PLAYED IN GERMANY'S EURO 2004 QUALIFYING GAMES? ★

LITHUANIA	FAROE ISLANDS	LITHUANIA	SCOTLAND	FAROE ISLANDS	ICELAND	SCOTLAND	ICELAND
Won 2-0 (a) *og	Won 2-1 (h)	Drew 1-1 (h)	Drew 1-1 (a)	Won 2-0 (a)	Drew 0-0 (a)	Won 2-1 (h)	Won 3-0 (h)
Kahn	Kahn	Kahn	Kahn	Kahn	Kahn	Kahn	Kahn
Linke	Friedrich	Friedrich	Friedrich	Friedrich	Friedrich	Friedrich	Friedrich
Ramelow	Ramelow	Rau	Rau	Rau	Rau	Rau	Hinkel
Metzelder	Worns	Worns	Worns	Worns	Worns	Worns	Worns
Frings	Frings	Frings	Frings	Freier	Baumann	Baumann	Baumann
Hamann	Hamann	Hamann	Jeremies	Kehl	Kehl	Rehmer	Rahn
Bohme	Jeremies	Ramelow 1	Ramelow	Ramelow	Ramelow	Ramelow	Ramelow
Ballack 1	Ballack 1	Bohme	Ballack	Jeremies	Ballack	Ballack 1	Ballack 1
Schneider	Schneider	Schneider	Schneider	Schneider	Schneider	Schneider	Schneider
Jancker	Jancker	Bobic	Bobic 1	Bobic 1	Klose	Bobic 1	Bobic 1
Klose	Klose 1	Klose	Klose	Neuville	Neuville	Kuranyi	Kuranyi 1
Substitutes:	*Substitutes:*	*Substitutes:*	*Substitutes:*	*Substitutes:*	*Substitutes:*	*Substitutes:*	*Substitutes:*
Neuville 69	Freier 46	Rehmer 46	Freier 56	Rost 46	Kuranyi 46	Klose 76	Klose 69
Jeremies 86	Neuville 68	Kuranyi 72	Neuville 74	Klose 1 65	Hartmann 61	Kehl 81	Neuville 85
	Kehl 86	Freier 82	Kehl 86	Hartmann 72	Deisler 69		

Arne Friedrich.

MATCHMAN'S VERDICT!

"Da Germans usually come good in da big tournaments, even if they've been pants before! But wiv da Czech Republic an' Holland in da same group as them, I can see an early exit. Laters!"

GROUP D
CZECH REPUBLIC
GERMANY
HOLLAND
LATVIA

HOLLAND

With Van Nistelrooy in attack, Holland will be a real threat!

Holland must create a good team spirit at Euro 2004!

★ THE QUALIFYING SQUAD ★

Goalkeepers

Edwin van der Sar
Club: Fulham
Age: 33 ★ Caps/Goals: 79/0

Ronald Waterreus
Club: PSV
Age: 33 ★ Caps/Goals: 6/0

Sander Westerveld
Club: Real Sociedad
Age: 29 ★ Caps/Goals: 6/0

Edwin van der Sar.

Defenders

Frank de Boer.

Kevin Hofland
Club: PSV
Age: 25 ★ Caps/Goals: 6/0

Andre Ooijer
Club: PSV
Age: 29 ★ Caps/Goals: 13/1

Michael Reiziger
Club: Barcelona
Age: 31 ★ Caps/Goals: 65/1

Wilfred Bouma
Club: PSV
Age: 25 ★ Caps/Goals: 8/0

Frank de Boer
Club: Rangers
Age: 34 ★ Caps/Goals: 109/13

Johnny Heitinga
Club: Ajax
Age: 20 ★ Caps/Goals: 1/0

Fernando Ricksen
Club: Rangers
Age: 27 ★ Caps/Goals: 12/0

Jaap Stam
Club: Lazio
Age: 31 ★ Caps/Goals: 58/3

Giovanni van Bronckhorst
Club: Arsenal
Age: 29 ★ Caps/Goals: 32/3

Midfielders

Phillip Cocu
Club: Barcelona
Age: 33 ★ Caps/Goals: 75/7

Edgar Davids
Club: Barcelona
Age: 31 ★ Caps/Goals: 61/6

Ronald de Boer
Club: Rangers
Age: 34 ★ Caps/Goals: 67/13

Marc Overmars
Club: Barcelona
Age: 31 ★ Caps/Goals: 80/16

Clarence Seedorf
Club: AC Milan
Age: 28 ★ Caps/Goals: 69/11

Clarence Seedorf.

Wesley Sneijder
Club: Ajax
Age: 20 ★ Caps/Goals: 4/2

Mark van Bommel
Club: PSV
Age: 27 ★ Caps/Goals: 23/5

Andy van der Meyde
Club: Inter Milan
Age: 24 ★ Caps/Goals: 9/1

Rafael van der Vaart
Club: Ajax
Age: 21 ★ Caps/Goals: 14/3

Boudewijn Zenden
Club: Chelsea
Age: 27 ★ Caps/Goals: 47/6

Boudewijn Zenden.

Strikers

Jimmy Floyd Hasselbaink
Club: Chelsea
Age: 32 ★ Caps/Goals: 23/9

Patrick Kluivert
Club: Barcelona
Age: 28 ★ Caps/Goals: 75/40

Roy Makaay
Club: Bayern Munich
Age: 29 ★ Caps/Goals: 27/3

Arjen Robben
Club: Chelsea
Age: 20 ★ Caps/Goals: 4/2

Pierre van Hooijdonk
Club: Fenerbahce
Age: 34 ★ Caps/Goals: 35/11

Ruud van Nistelrooy
Club: Man. United
Age: 28 ★ Caps/Goals: 30/14

Patrick Kluivert.

They reached Euro 2004 via the play-offs, but HOLLAND could go a long way this summer!

HOW DID THEY QUALIFY?

It was a straight fight between Holland and the Czech Republic to see who topped their qualifying group. In the end it was the Dutch who had to go into the play-offs after a 3-1 defeat to the Czechs in September 2003. They faced Scotland over two legs, and despite a 1-0 defeat in Glasgow, a fantastic 6-0 win in Amsterdam assured their Euro 2004 place!

WHAT ARE HOLLAND'S STRENGTHS?

The squad is packed with quality and experience. Kluivert, Davids, Seedorf, Van der Sar and the De Boers all played together at Ajax and have been international team-mates for years. Add others like Stam, Van Nistelrooy, Overmars, Van der Meyde and Van der Vaart, and it's a strong squad with versatile players who can easily change formation.

AND THEIR WEAKNESSES?

Dick Advocaat doesn't know who his first-choice defence will be, or the team's best formation. Frank de Boer should start next to Stam, but he's had an unsettled season with Galatasaray and Rangers. If Holland play three at the back, then Seedorf and Zenden could play as the wing-backs, but in a back four, Zenden, Cocu or Bouma could go to left-back. Either way, they lack real quality in defence.

HOW WILL THEY DO?

Holland's reputation improved after their 6-0 crushing of Scotland, and many fancy them to make at least the semi-finals. With brilliant creative and attacking talent they'll be great to watch, but against well-drilled teams like England and Italy, they may struggle. It'll be great to have the Dutch and their mad fans at the finals, and maybe they can go all the way – like when they won it in 1988!

★ HOLLAND'S STRONGEST LINE-UP ★

VAN DER SAR

REIZIGER — STAM — F DE BOER — BOUMA

VAN DER MEYDE — DAVIDS — COCU — VAN DER VAART

VAN NISTELROOY — KLUIVERT

★ FINAL QUALIFYING TABLE ★

TEAM	P	W	D	L	F	A	PTS
1. CZECH REPUBLIC	**8**	**7**	**1**	**0**	**23**	**5**	**22**
2. HOLLAND	8	6	1	1	20	6	19
3. AUSTRIA	8	3	0	5	12	14	9
4. MOLDOVA	8	2	0	6	5	19	6
5. BELARUS	8	1	0	7	4	20	3

The Dutch beat Scotland in the play-offs.

HOLLAND STATS & FACTS!

MANAGER: Dick Advocaat

CAPTAIN: Frank de Boer

MOST CAPS (Current Squad):
Frank de Boer, 109

MOST GOALS (Qualifying):
Ruud van Nistelrooy, 5

WORLD RANKING: 4th

ODDS TO WIN EURO 2004: 7/1

PREVIOUS TOURNAMENTS

EURO 2000: Semi-finals

BEST EVER: Winners, 1988

KNVB

★ HOLLAND'S STAR MEN ★

JAAP STAM ★ Defender

Frank de Boer has twice as many caps as Stam, but the powerful Lazio centre-back is Holland's most reliable defender. Whether playing in a back three or an attack-minded back four, the 31-year-old ex-Man. United star has the experience and ability to keep Europe's top strikers quiet. Expected to retire from the international scene after the finals.

EDGAR DAVIDS ★ Midfielder

A big favourite of coach Dick Advocaat, 'The Pitbull' went to Barça on loan from Juventus this year to get regular games ahead of the finals. The left-footed ace has competition for a starting place, but his will-to-win and huge experience will be vital if Holland want to have any chance of success in Portugal.

RUUD VAN NISTELROOY ★ Striker

The Man. United star goes into the finals full of confidence after another great season at Old Trafford. He's had some problems with Dick Advocaat, but Ruud should lead the attack with Patrick Kluivert, and anyone who saw his awesome hat-trick against Scotland in the play-offs will know he's a lethal striker!

★ WHO PLAYED IN HOLLAND'S EURO 2004 QUALIFYING GAMES? ★

BELARUS		AUSTRIA		CZECH REP.		MOLDOVA		BELARUS		AUSTRIA		CZECH REP.		MOLDOVA		SCOTLAND		SCOTLAND	
Won 3-0 (h)		*Won 3-0 (a)*		*Drew 1-1 (h)*		*Won 2-1 (a)*		*Won 2-0 (a)*		*Won 3-1 (h)*		*Lost 3-1 (a)*		*Won 5-0 (h)*		*Lost 1-0 (a)*		*Won 6-0 (h)*	
Van der Sar		Van der Sar		Waterreus		Waterreus		Van der Sar		Van der Saar		Van der Sar		Van der Saar		Van der Sar		Van der Saar	
Ricksen		Ricksen		Ricksen		Reiziger		Reiziger		Reiziger		Reiziger		Reiziger		Ooijer		Ooijer 1	
Cocu		Cocu 1		Van Bronckhorst		Zenden		Van Bronckhorst		Cocu 1		Cocu		Van Bronckhorst		Van Bronckhorst		Bouma	
F. De Boer		F. De Boer		F. De Boer		F. De Boer		F. De Boer		F. De Boer		F. De Boer		Ooijer		F. De Boer		Cocu	
Stam		Stam		Stam		Stam		Stam		Stam		Stam		Stam		Stam		Reiziger	
Zenden		Zenden		Zenden		Van der Vaart		Zenden		Zenden		Overmars		Overmars		Overmars		Sneijder 1	
Van Bommel		Van Bommel		Van Bommel		Van Bommel 1		Van Bommel		Van Bommel		Van Bommel		Sneijder 1		Cocu		Davids	
Davids 1		Davids		Davids		Davids		Cocu		Davids		Davids		Cocu		Davids		Van der Meyde	
Van der Meyde		Seedorf 1		Seedorf		Seedorf		Seedorf		Van der Meyde		Van der Vaart 1		Van der Meyde		Van der Meyde		Van Nistelrooy	
Van Nistelrooy		Makaay 1		Van Nistelrooy 1		Van Nistelrooy 1		Van Nistelrooy		Van der Vaart 1		Van Nistelrooy		Van der Vaart 1		Van Nistelrooy		Van Nistelrooy 3	
Kluivert 1		Kluivert		Kluivert		Kluivert		Kluivert 1		Kluivert 1		Kluivert		Kluivert 1		Kluivert		Van der Vaart	
Substitutes:		*Substitutes:*		*Substitutes:*		*Substitutes:*		*Substitutes:*		*Substitutes:*		*Substitutes:*		*Substitutes:*		*Substitutes:*		*Substitutes:*	
Van der Vaart	69	Bouma	76	Van der Vaart	39	Ricksen	64	Bosvelt	46	Overmars	46	Bosvelt	20	Makaay	32	Seedorf	45	F. De Boer 1	46
Hasselbaink 1	69	R. De Boer	76	Makaay	81	R. De Boer	66	Overmars 1	61	Van Hooijdonk	46	Van Hooijdonk	69	Robben 1	68	Van der Vaart	66	Seedorf	67
Reiziger	81	Hasselbaink	80			Van Hooijdonk	75	Van der Vaart	76	Robben	71			Van Hooijdonk 1 71		Makaay	77	Kluivert	76

GROUP D
CZECH REPUBLIC
GERMANY
HOLLAND
LATVIA

LATVIA

★ THE QUALIFYING SQUAD ★

Goalkeepers

Alex Kolinko
Club: FC Rostov
Age: 28 ★ Caps/Goals: 46/0

Andrejs Piedels
Club: Skonto Riga
Age: 33 ★ Caps/Goals: 5/0

Andris Vanins
Club: Torpedo-Metallurg
Age: 24 ★ Caps/Goals: 4/0

Alex Kolinko.

Defenders

Igor Stepanovs.

Igors Korablovs
Club: Ventspills
Age: 29 ★ Caps/Goals: 11/0

Valentins Lobanovs
Club: Skonto Riga
Age: 32 ★ Caps/Goals: 44/1

Vadim Login
Club: Skonto Riga
Age: 22 ★ Caps/Goals: 0/0

Olegs Blagonadezdins
Club: Alania Vladikavkaz
Age: 31 ★ Caps/Goals: 62/2

Igors Stepanovs
Club: Beveren
Age: 28 ★ Caps/Goals: 66/3

Aleksandrs Isakovs
Club: Skonto Riga
Age: 30 ★ Caps/Goals: 40/0

Mihails Zemlinskis
Club: Skonto Riga
Age: 34 ★ Caps/Goals: 92/8

Deniss Ivanovs
Club: Liepajas Metalurgs
Age: 20 ★ Caps/Goals: 0/0

Dzintars Zirnis
Club: Liepajas Metalurgs
Age: 27 ★ Caps/Goals: 16/0

Midfielders

Vitalis Astafjevs
Club: Admira-Wacker
Age: 33 ★ Caps/Goals: 99/10

Kristaps Blanks
Club: Skonto Riga
Age: 18 ★ Caps/Goals: 4/0

Inmants Bleidelis
Club: Viborg
Age: 28 ★ Caps/Goals: 76/8

Vladimirs Kolesnicenko
Club: Torpedo-Metallurg
Age: 23 ★ Caps/Goals: 26/3

Jurijs Laizans
Club: CSKA Moscow
Age: 25 ★ Caps/Goals: 51/7

Vitalis Astafjevs.

Jurgis Pucinskis
Club: Shinnik Yaroslav
Age: 31 ★ Caps/Goals: 14/0

Andrejs Rubins
Club: Shinnik Yaroslav
Age: 25 ★ Caps/Goals: 52/6

Igors Semjonovs
Club: Skonto Riga
Age: 18 ★ Caps/Goals: 6/0

Andrejs Stolcers
Club: Fulham
Age: 29 ★ Caps/Goals: 73/7

Inmants Bleidelis.

Strikers

Viktors Dobrecovs
Club: Liepajas Metalurgs
Age: 27 ★ Caps/Goals: 15/0

Girts Karlsons
Club: Shinnik Yaroslav
Age: 23 ★ Caps/Goals: 3/0

Mihails Miholaps
Club: Alania Vladikavkaz
Age: 29 ★ Caps/Goals: 26/2

Marian Pahars
Club: Southampton
Age: 27 ★ Caps/Goals: 58/15

Andrejs Prohorenkovs
Club: Maccabi Tel-Aviv
Age: 27 ★ Caps/Goals: 7/1

Vits Rimkus
Club: Ventspils
Age: 30 ★ Caps/Goals: 43/8

Maris Verpakovskis
Club: Dynamo Kiev
Age: 24 ★ Caps/Goals: 29/10

Vits Rimkus.

Latvia beat Sweden on their way to Euro 2004.

*Rank outsiders **LATVIA** hope to cause an upset in their first ever European Championships!*

HOW DID THEY QUALIFY?

Latvia reached Euro 2004 via the back door after finishing second in their group and winning a play-off with Turkey. Their first four games went well, picking up three wins and a draw, but defeats to Hungary and Poland set them back. Coach Aleksandrs Starkovs turned things around though, with wins over Hungary and Sweden to set up that play-off with Turkey. Latvia won 3-2 on aggregate to reach their first ever Euro finals!

WHAT ARE LATVIA'S STRENGTHS?

They've learnt how to play international footy, which is important! The former Soviet state only has about 100 pro players in its eight-team league, but with key players now operating in stronger leagues around Europe, Latvia are getting better. The coach has got them playing counter-attacking football and it's working.

AND THEIR WEAKNESSES?

After scoring six goals in qualifying, star striker Maris Verpakovskis has now become Latvia's Golden Boy – even overtaking Marian Pahars as his country's main man in attack. There's no doubt the 24-year-old is a big talent, but the danger is that if he's not firing, Latvia will struggle to score goals. Verpakovskis also made a big move to Dynamo Kiev in January, and coach Starkovs hopes this will improve him further – and not unsettle his star before the finals start.

HOW WILL THEY DO?

At 500/1 Latvia are the rank outsiders to lift the Euro 2004 trophy, but they've done the hard part in reaching the finals! It's the first time the country has ever qualified for a big tournament – and they've been drawn in a group with the Czech Republic, Germany and Holland! But they'll still enjoy themselves – even if they lose every single game!

★ LATVIA'S STRONGEST LINE-UP ★

KOLINKO

ZIRNIS — STEPANOVS — ZEMLINSKIS — BLAGONADEZDINS

BLEIDELIS — LAIZANS — ASTAFJEVS — RUBINS

PAHARS — VERPAKOVSKIS

The Latvians celebrate on their way to Euro 2004!

★ FINAL QUALIFYING TABLE ★

TEAM	P	W	D	L	F	A	PTS
1. SWEDEN	8	5	2	1	19	3	17
2. LATVIA	8	5	1	2	10	6	16
3. POLAND	8	4	1	3	11	7	13
4. HUNGARY	8	3	2	3	15	9	11
5. SAN MARINO	8	0	0	8	0	30	0

Latvia finished runners-up in their qualifying group.

LATVIA STATS & FACTS!

MANAGER: Aleksandrs Starkovs

CAPTAIN: Vitalis Astafjevs

MOST CAPS (Current Squad):
Vitalis Astafjevs, 99

MOST GOALS (Qualifying):
Maris Verpakovskis, 6

WORLD RANKING: 53rd

ODDS TO WIN EURO 2004: 500/1

PREVIOUS TOURNAMENTS

EURO 2000: Did Not Qualify

BEST EVER: Never Qualified Before

★ LATVIA'S STAR MEN ★

ALEX KOLINKO ★ Goalkeeper

You may remember Kolinko as the man Trevor Francis clipped around the ear when he was at Crystal Palace, but after moving to Russia, the Latvia No.1 has hit top form again. The 28-year-old stopper played in all ten Euro 2004 qualifiers – keeping six clean sheets – and goes into the finals full of confidence.

ANDREJS RUBINS ★ Midfielder

Rubins never really did the business during his two-year spell at Crystal Palace, but he's now enjoying his footy in the Russian league and is the first-choice left-winger for Latvia. Pacy and direct, the 25-year-old ace loves bombing forward to whip in crosses, and started all ten of the Euro 2004 qualifiers.

MARIAN PAHARS ★ Striker

The silky Southampton forward only started three qualifiers because of injury, but after battling back to full fitness, he's hoping to rediscover his magic touch for his country. Pahars should start in attack with the in-form Maris Verpakovskis, or he could play on the wing as he often does for The Saints, with Vits Rimkus being the second striker.

MATCHMAN'S VERDICT!

"Latvia? Where da 'eck is dat? Whatever, I is already a Latvia fan coz I is lovin' how dis tiny team made it to Euro 2004! They could get an ass-whuppin' big style, but nuff respect!"

★ WHO PLAYED IN LATVIA'S EURO 2004 QUALIFYING GAMES? ★

SWEDEN	POLAND	SAN MARINO	SAN MARINO	HUNGARY	POLAND	HUNGARY	SWEDEN	TURKEY	TURKEY
Drew 0-0 (h)	*Won 1-0 (a)*	*Won 1-0 (a) *og*	*Won 3-0 (h)*	*Lost 3-1 (a)*	*Lost 2-0 (h)*	*Won 3-1 (h)*	*Won 1-0 (a)*	*Won 1-0 (h)*	*Drew 2-2 (a)*
Kolinko	Kolinko	Kolinko	Kolinko	Kolinko	Kolinko	Kolinko	Kolinko	Kolinko	Kolinko
Blagonadezdins	Blagonadezdins	Blagonadezdins	Zirnis	Blagonadezdins	Blagonadezdins	Zirnis	Zirnis	Korablovs	Zirnis
Isakovs	Isakovs	Isakovs	Isakovs	Isakovs	Isakovs	Blagonadezdins	Blagonadezdins	Isakovs	Isakovs
Stepanovs	Stepanovs	Stepanovs	Stepanovs	Stepanovs	Stepanovs	Stepanovs	Stepanovs	Stepanovs	Stepanovs
Zemlinskis	Zemlinskis	Zemlinskis	Zemlinskis	Zemlinskis	Zemlinskis	Zemlinskis	Zemlinskis	Lobanovs	Zemlinskis
Laizans	Laizans 1	Ko?esnicenko	Laizans	Laizans	Lobanovs	Lobanovs	Lobanovs	Laizans	Laizans 1
Astafjevs	Astafjevs	Astafjevs	Miholaps	Astafjevs	Lobanovs	Astafjevs	Astafjevs	Astafjevs	Astafjevs
Bleidelis	Bleidelis	Bleidelis	Bleidelis 2	Bleidelis	Bleidelis	Bleidelis 1	Bleidelis	Bleidelis	Bleidelis
Rubins	Rubins	Rubins	Rubins	Rubins	Rubins	Rubins	Rubins	Rubins	Rubins
Verpakovskis	Verpakovskis	Verpakovskis	Verpakovskis	Lobanovs	Verpakovskis	Verpakovskis 2	Verpakovskis 1	Verpakovskis 1	Verpakovskis
Pahars	Pahars	Pahars	Prohorenkovs 1	Verpakovskis 1	Prohorenkovs	Rimkus	Rimkus	Rimkus	Rimkus
Substitutes:	*Substitutes:*	*Substitutes:*	*Substitutes:*	*Substitutes:*	*Substitutes:*	*Substitutes:*	*Substitutes:*	*Substitutes:*	*Substitutes:*
Stolcers 80	Prohorenkovs 58	Stolcers 46	Rimkus 60	Semjonovs 75	Semjonovs 76	Semjonovs 75	Isakovs 75	Pucinskis 82	Stolcers 79
	Stolcers 89	Prohorenkovs 57	Stolcers 79	Kolesnicenko 89	Rimkus 79	Kolesnicenko 89	Pucinskis 80	Stolcers 86	Pahars 89
		Miholaps 64	Dobrecovs 85		Stolcers 82		Stolcers 89	Kolesnicenko 89	

DID YOU KNOW...?

UEFA STRUGGLED TO FIND 16 TEAMS TO PLAY IN THE FIRST EVER EUROPEAN CHAMPIONSHIPS, AND NONE OF THE HOME NATIONS ENTERED AT ALL!

OI, UEFA! YOU CAN STUFF YER EURO CHAMPIONSHIPS, RIGHT?

MOUNTAIN FOOTY!

This Euro 2004 stadium in Braga is built into the side of a mountain! You'll see it when Latvia play Holland and Denmark do battle with Bulgaria!

EURO DREAM

The best of the best will be strutting their stuff at Euro 2004 as some of the world's wickedest players come face to face in Portugal! But imagine if all the European stars could play in the same team – who would make it into your starting XI? Check out the MATCH Euro Dream Team, then write your own Dream XI in the boxes below. Nice one!

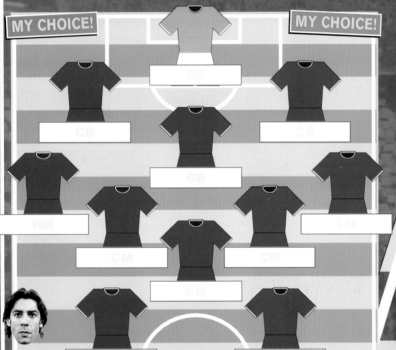

MY CHOICE!   MY CHOICE!

GK
CB   CB
CB
RM   LM
CM   CM
CM
S   S

MY SUBSTITUTES!

CB   S
GK
M   S

FIGO
PORTUGAL

HENRY
FRANCE

THURAM
FRANCE

BECKHAM
ENGLAND

5
OLD TIMERS!

Fernando Couto
Portugal ★ Age: 34

Victor Onopko
Russia ★ Age: 34

Rene Henriksen
Denmark ★ Age: 34

Oliver Kahn
Germany ★ Age: 34

Marcel Desailly
France ★ Age: 35

TEAM!

BUFFON
ITALY

CAMPBELL
ENGLAND

SUBSTITUTES

CASILLAS
SPAIN

STAM
HOLLAND

BALLACK
GERMANY

RAUL
SPAIN

VIERI
ITALY

NESTA
ITALY

ZIDANE
FRANCE

VIEIRA
FRANCE

NEDVED
CZECH REPUBLIC

VAN NISTELROOY
HOLLAND

COUNTING THE COSTA!
There were 20 Rui Costas hiding throughout Planet Football. Did you manage to find them all?

TEST YER TRUE FOOTY KNOWLEDGE IN DA FIRST 'ALF OF ME WICKED EURO 2004 QUIZ, DUDES!

PERCY'S Twue or Fwalse!

HELP ME TO LEARN ABOUT FWOOTY BY TICKING WHICH OF THESE FACTS ARE TWUE AND CWOSSING WHICH ARE FWALSE!

1. Sylvain Wiltord plays for Sweden!
2. Patrick Vieira was born in Senegal!
3. Euro 2004 is being held in Spain!
4. Mikael Silvestre is a defender!
5. Michael Owen is a striker!

2 POINTS FOR EACH CORRECT ANSWER **MY SCORE** /10

TEAM QUIZ - PORTUGAL!

SEE 'OW MUCH YA REALLY KNOW ABOUT WICKED EURO 2004 HOSTS, PORTUGAL! GO ON, 'AVE A GO!

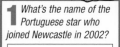

1 What's the name of the Portuguese star who joined Newcastle in 2002?

2 Which top Portuguese player wears the No.10 shirt for Real Madrid?

3 Fulham signed Luis Boa Morte from which Premiership club in 2001?

4 Portugal are in Group A along with Spain, Russia and which other team?

5 What's the name of Barcelona's Portuguese star with the initials 'RQ'?

2 POINTS FOR EACH CORRECT ANSWER **MY SCORE** /10

DANISH BACON OR SWISS CHEESE?

1. BERNT HAAS 2. JESPER GRONKJAER 3. THOMAS GRAVESEN 4. STEPHANE HENCHOZ 5. THOMAS SORENSEN

ANSWER   ANSWER   ANSWER   ANSWER   ANSWER

SCRIBBLE 'BACON' NEXT TO DA DANISH FOOTY PLAYERS AN' 'CHEESE' NEXT TO DA SWISS ONES! THERE'S 10 POINTS UP FOR GRABS 'ERE!

2 POINTS FOR EACH CORRECT ANSWER **MY SCORE** /10

SPANISH STARS!

JOIN UP DA SPANISH FOOTY PLAYERS WITH DA LA LIGA TEAMS THEY PLAY FOR!

1. JUAN CARLOS VALERON — A ATLETICO MADRID
2. SANTIAGO CANIZARES — B REAL BETIS
3. FERNANDO TORRES — C DEPORTIVO LA CORUNA
4. JOAQUIN — D REAL MADRID
5. RAUL — E VALENCIA

2 POINTS FOR EACH CORRECT ANSWER **MY SCORE** /10

dream team!

FIGURE OUT DA CLUES TO REVEAL A TEAM O' PREM STARS WHO COULD BE MIXIN' IT UP IN PORTUGAL DIS SUMMER! I'VE GIVEN YA ONE TO START WITH!

Aston Villa and Denmark No.1!

GK ANSWER

England star at Middlesbrough! | Experienced Swiss star at Anfield! | Villa's big beardy Swede! | Pacy England and Arsenal man!

RB ANSWER | **CB** ANSWER | **CB** ANSWER | **LB** Ashley Cole

Man. United's Portugal wonderkid! | Russia ace on loan at Pompey! | Liverpool's skilful 'Czech' mate! | Dutch winger who starred for Boro!

RM ANSWER | **CM** ANSWER | **CM** ANSWER | **LM** ANSWER

Spanish ace at Arsenal! | England and Everton youngster!

S ANSWER | **S** ANSWER

1 POINT FOR EACH CORRECT ANSWER **MY SCORE** /10

QUIZ!

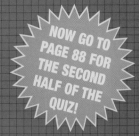

GROUND FORCE!

ANSWER

WHICH PORTUGUESE CLUB PLAY AT DA WICKED DRAGAO STADIUM?

10 POINTS FOR CORRECT ANSWER

MY SCORE /10

CAP COUNTER!

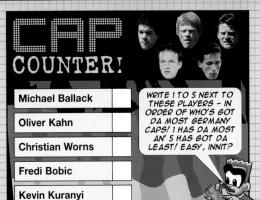

Michael Ballack	
Oliver Kahn	
Christian Worns	
Fredi Bobic	
Kevin Kuranyi	

WRITE 1 TO 5 NEXT TO THESE PLAYERS – IN ORDER OF WHO'S GOT DA MOST GERMANY CAPS! 1 HAS DA MOST AN' 5 HAS GOT DA LEAST! EASY, INNIT?

2 POINTS FOR EACH CORRECT ANSWER

MY SCORE /10

WHO AM I?

CAN YA FIGURE OUT WHICH PLAYER IS HIDDEN UNDER DA FACE OF EURO 2004 MASCOT, KINAS?

ANSWER

> I was born on February 11, 1983!
> My first name sounds like a Teenage Mutant Ninja Turtle!
> I play for Ajax and Holland!

10 POINTS FOR CORRECT ANSWER

MY SCORE /10

ULTIMATE CHALLENGE!

'AVE A CRACK AT DIS QUICK TEN-QUESTION EURO CHAMPS TEASER! JUS' SCRIBBLE YER ANSWERS IN DA BOXES BELOW, AN' SEE IF YA GET MAXIMUM POINTS!

1 Which colourful team beat Scotland over two legs in the Euro 2004 play-offs to make this summer's finals? ANSWER

2 Which country lifted the European Championship trophy in 2000 with a Golden Goal winner? ANSWER

3 And who did they beat in dramatic fashion in the final that year? ANSWER

4 If a knockout game in Euro 2004 is level after 90 minutes, will there be 'Golden Goal' or 'Silver Goal' rules? ANSWER

5 How many times have the Czech Republic won the European Championships? ANSWER

6 Which highly-rated team did Latvia beat in the play-offs to make it through to the finals of Euro 2004? ANSWER

7 Are Bulgaria in Group A or Group C at this summer's European Championships? ANSWER

8 How many footy stadiums will be used in Euro 2004? Is it five, eight or ten? ANSWER

9 'The Azzurri' is the nickname for which top team at this summer's European Championships? ANSWER

10 When was the last time Germany won the European Championships? ANSWER

1 POINT FOR EACH CORRECT ANSWER   MY SCORE /10

SORT THE KIT OUT!

WHICH FOOTY BRANDS MAKE THESE CLASSY KITS? MATCH 'EM UP IF YA CAN!

1 ITALY	2 ENGLAND	3 HOLLAND KNVB	4 GERMANY	5 DENMARK DBU 1889

A UMBRO	B ADIDAS	C PUMA	D HUMMEL	E NIKE

2 POINTS FOR EACH CORRECT ANSWER

MY SCORE /10

ANSWERS

20 STARS TO AT EURO

We all know about Beckham, Zidane and Figo — but who are the next generation of superstars to watch at Euro 2004? **MATCH** checks out 20 of Europe's most promising youngsters, as they get ready to rock this summer's tournament!

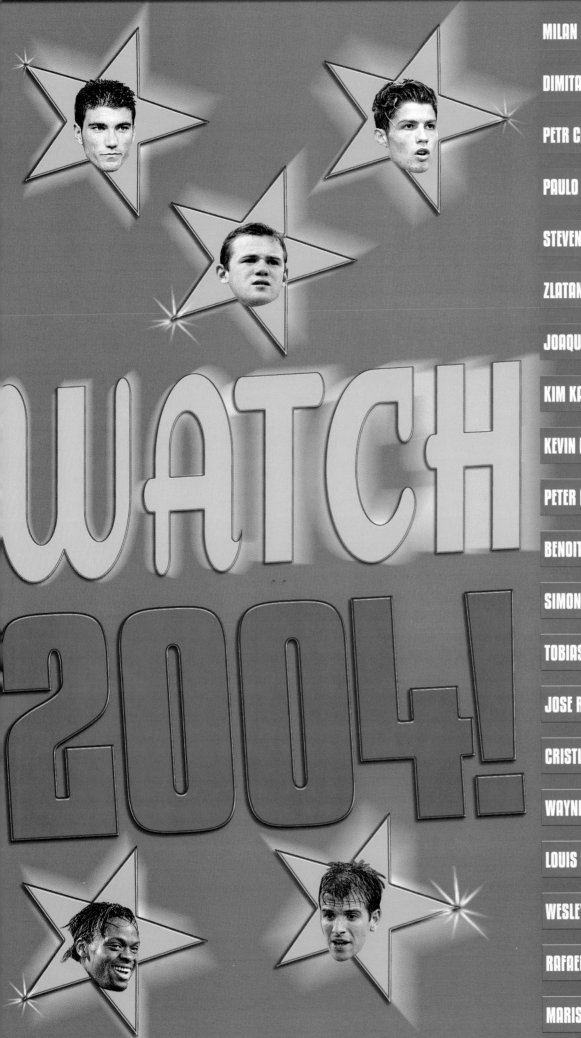

WATCH 2004!

EURO 2004
STARS TO WATCH!

★ MILAN BAROS ★

>> **Liverpool** >> **Czech Republic**
>> **Age: 22** >> **Position: Striker**

After missing five months of the season with a broken leg, Milan Baros is raring to go at Euro 2004! That long spell on the sidelines means he's refreshed and ready to continue his excellent record at international level. The Liverpool striker netted on his Czech Republic debut and hasn't stopped scoring since, hitting 12 goals in 21 games for his country – despite starting on the bench in many of those games! Quick, strong and skilful, Baros doesn't muck around on the ball, he heads straight for goal – and that's a nightmare for even the best defender!

EURO 2004
STARS TO WATCH!

★ DIMITAR BERBATOV ★

>> **Bayer Leverkusen** >> **Bulgaria**
>> **Age: 23** >> **Position: Striker**

Bulgaria are back on the international scene big time after struggling in recent years, and Dimitar Berbatov is leading the charge! The 23-year-old striker was crucial to Bulgaria's qualifying campaign, hitting five priceless goals to finish as the team's top goalscorer. He also goes to the Euro 2004 finals after helping his German club Bayer Leverkusen to a much-improved position in the Bundesliga. With an already impressive international goalscoring record of 15 goals in 27 games, Berbatov is ready to take the tournament by storm!

EURO 2004
STARS TO WATCH!

★ PETR CECH ★

>> **Chelsea** >> **Czech Republic**
>> **Age: 22** >> **Position: Goalkeeper**

Don't be surprised if Chelsea fans take a special interest in the Czech Republic at Euro 2004 – they'll be checking out their new goalkeeper! Cech will move to Stamford Bridge when the tournament ends, after French club Rennes finally agreed to sell him him for £9 million – so he has a big transfer fee, and a big reputation, to justify. Standing 6ft 5ins, it won't be too difficult to spot him in a crowded penalty area, and he won't go flapping around either – for a young international 'keeper, he's super-cool and a real star to watch this summer!

★ PAULO FERREIRA ★

>> **Porto** >> **Portugal**
>> **Age: 25** >> **Position: Defender**

The 25-year-old Porto right-back was named ahead of both Michel Salgado and Lilian Thuram in UEFA's 2003 Team Of The Year after winning the Portuguese league, Portuguese Cup and UEFA Cup – so it's no surprise Europe's top clubs are sniffing around Ferreira with their chequebooks ready. The athletic defender caused Man. United loads of problems with his attacking runs in the Champions League this season, but Sir Alex Ferguson will face stiff competition for his signature if Ferreira has a good Euro 2004!

EURO 2004
STARS TO WATCH!

★ STEVEN GERRARD ★

>> **Liverpool** >> **England**
>> **Age: 24** >> **Position: Midfielder**

It's been four long years since Steven Gerrard played in a major tournament with England. So that, combined with missing the World Cup through injury, has made him desperate for success at international level. Taking the captain's armband at Liverpool has helped him to mature as a player, and he's become a key member of Sven Goran Eriksson's team with his huge midfield engine, fantastic passing range, rocket shot and rock-hard tackles. One thing's for sure, watching him in action with England this summer will be worth the wait!

EURO 2004
STARS TO WATCH!

★ ZLATAN IBRAHIMOVIC ★

>> **Ajax** >> **Sweden**

>> **Age: 22** >> **Position: Striker**

Bad news: Henrik Larsson has retired. Good news: Zlatan Ibrahimovic will take his place! After deputising for Larsson at the World Cup, the 22-year-old will be Sweden's main striker this summer. He'll be keen to prove his goalscoring skill and technique, but hopefully he'll leave his temper at home! Sometimes selfish, but always exciting on the ball, the tall Ajax star has been chased by Italian giants Roma for a couple of years. Euro 2004 is his chance to put himself in the shop window and finally get that big-money move to a top club!

EURO 2004
STARS TO WATCH!

★ JOAQUIN ★

>> **Real Betis** >> **Spain**
>> **Age: 22** >> **Position: Midfielder**

If you believe the rumours, Joaquin will join either Real Madrid or Man. United in the summer – as a replacement for Luis Figo, or to fill the gap that's been left by David Beckham at Old Trafford! The 22-year-old winger is brilliant to watch with the ball at his feet – he's a gifted dribbler who teases defenders before leaving them for dead, and he was in great goalscoring form for Real Betis this season. He'll have to watch his temper with Spain at Euro 2004, because he can be a bit of a hothead, but we can't wait to see him in action!

EURO 2004
STARS TO WATCH!

★ KIM KALLSTROM ★

>> **Rennes** >> **Sweden**

>> **Age: 21** >> **Position: Midfielder**

This year could be a massive one for Kim Kallstrom, who's hoping to make a real impact in Sweden's midfield at Euro 2004. There's been a buzz about the 21-year-old ever since he began his career with Swedish side Djurgardens, and this tournament gives him the ideal chance to show what all the hype has been about. Now playing a starring role for Rennes in France, Kallstrom is a two-footed, attacking central midfielder. He scored his first senior goal against San Marino in qualifying and now he's set to become Sweden's No.1 playmaker!

EURO 2004
STARS TO WATCH!

★ KEVIN KURANYI ★

Stuttgart   Germany
Age: 22   Position: Striker

Born in Brazil, made in Germany, Kevin Kuranyi has come from nowhere two years ago to become one of the most lethal strikers in the Bundesliga and his nation's most promising centre-forward. Having helped Stuttgart to runners-up in the Bundesliga in 2002-03, scoring 15 goals, Kuranyi transferred his skills to the Champions League this season and struck a memorable winner against Man. United, as well as strikes against Rangers and Panathinaikos. Europe's top clubs are watching Kuranyi, who's quality in the air and neat on the deck!

EURO 2004
STARS TO WATCH!

★ PETER LOVENKRANDS ★

>> **Rangers** >> **Denmark**
>> **Age: 24** >> **Position: Striker**

Denmark have loads of good attacking options, so it's lucky that Lovenkrands can play as a left-winger or a striker because he'll be desperate to make a major impact at Euro 2004. Mainly used as a substitute at the World Cup, the 24-year-old should play a bigger role this time. His tricky runs down the left, coupled with his eye for goal – he famously scored a brilliant Scottish Cup final winner for Rangers against Celtic in 2002 – will give Denmark's Group C opponents Italy, Sweden and Bulgaria a few sleepless nights this June!

EURO 2004
STARS TO WATCH!

★ BENOIT PEDRETTI ★

>> Sochaux >> France
>> Age: 23 >> Position: Midfielder

If you haven't seen Pedretti play before, he's just like a French version of Steven Gerrard – with a never-say-die attitude and an excellent passing range from midfield. He was a regular when France claimed the Confederations Cup last summer, and he could have a big part to play at Euro 2004 as a deputy to Patrick Vieira. The 23-year-old Sochaux skipper is a massive star in the French league and has already turned down moves to PSG and Marseille – but watch out for a big-money move to a leading European side after the tournament!

EURO 2004
STARS TO WATCH!

★ TOBIAS RAU ★

Bayern Munich   Germany
Age: 22   Position: Defender

This promising defender started his career as a teenager at Bundesliga side Wolfsburg, but he soon became a target for Bayern Munich and signed for the German giants last summer. Rau has been converted from a midfielder to a left-back but still loves to get forward and put dangerous crosses into the box. He made his Germany debut against Spain, scored in his third game, and is now first choice at either left-back or left wing-back. One thing to watch out for is his diving, though – he hits the deck faster than Ronaldo eats pies!

EURO 2004
STARS TO WATCH!

★ JOSE ANTONIO REYES ★

>> **Arsenal** >> **Spain**

>> **Age: 20** >> **Position: Striker**

Arsene Wenger doesn't splash his cash very often, so spending £17 million on a 20-year-old must make Jose Antonio Reyes pretty special! Reyes can play on the wing, where he terrorises defenders with his pace and wicked dribbling, but his future at Arsenal will be up front with Thierry Henry. The Spain squad has some superb attacking players, but Reyes has already made an impressive start to his international career. He scored two goals in his first four games for Spain, and could prove too good to leave out of the team at Euro 2004!

EURO 2004
STARS TO WATCH!

★ CRISTIANO RONALDO ★

>> **Man. United** >> **Portugal**
>> **Age: 19** >> **Position: Midfielder**

Move over Luis Figo, there's a new king of the stepovers and his name is Ronaldo! The £12 million winger has already won over the Man. United fans with his pace, trickery and dazzling skills, and now he's ready to star for hosts Portugal at Euro 2004. He's not guaranteed a place in the starting line-up, but neither was Michael Owen when he made his tournament debut at the 1998 World Cup – and look what happened then! Portugal's final group game against rivals Spain will be huge, so that's Ronaldo's big chance to shine!

EURO 2004
STARS TO WATCH!

★ WAYNE ROONEY ★

>> **Everton** >> **England**

>> **Age: 18** >> **Position: Striker**

England fans are hoping to see the best of Wayne Rooney at Euro 2004, where he'll make his major tournament debut. The Everton wonderkid had a fairly quiet season after bursting on to the scene in 2002-03, but he always looks a class act for England. After making his debut as a substitute against Australia, he was sensational in his first start against Turkey, and his strike partnership with Michael Owen already looks special! This will be Europe's first glimpse of Roonaldo – they'll see awesome control, electric speed and a thunderbolt shot!

EURO 2004
STARS TO WATCH!

★ LOUIS SAHA ★

>> **Man. United** >> **France**
>> **Age: 25** >> **Position: Striker**

This time last year, Louis Saha finished a disappointing season at Fulham with just five league goals, but in the last 12 months he's scored over 20 goals and moved to Man. United for £12.8 million! Injury had affected the striker in past seasons, but it all clicked for him in 2003-04 and his brilliant form led to his first France call-up. And Saha didn't disappoint on his debut, scoring in the 2-0 friendly win against Belgium. With his lightning pace and silky skills, the classy striker could have a big role to play as France chase Euro 2004 glory!

EURO 2004
STARS TO WATCH!

★ WESLEY SNEIJDER ★

>> **Ajax** >> **Holland**
>> **Age: 20** >> **Position: Midfielder**

Wesley Sneijder is a man in a hurry.
The midfielder only made his club debut
for Ajax in February 2003 but then
made his international bow a couple
of months later – and by the end of the
year he was tearing poor Scotland apart
in the Euro 2004 play-offs! Sneijder
scored the first goal to pave the way
for a 6-0 victory for the Dutch, which
booked their place at this summer's
tournament. Dick Advocaat has loads
of talented players to squeeze into his
Holland squad, but he's sure to find
room for wicked Wesley somehow!

EURO 2004
STARS TO WATCH!

★ RAFAEL VAN DER VAART ★

>> **Ajax** >> **Holland**
>> **Age: 21** >> **Position: Midfielder**

While England still can't find a decent left-footed midfielder, Holland have no such worries – they've got Rafael van der Vaart. He shot to fame in the 2002-03 season, scoring 18 goals as Ajax finished runners-up in the Dutch league and reached the Champions League quarter-finals. But he actually made his full Holland debut back in 2001, and held down a regular place in the side during the final Euro 2004 qualifiers – scoring against Moldova, the Czech Republic and Austria. The 21-year-old is one to watch, for sure!

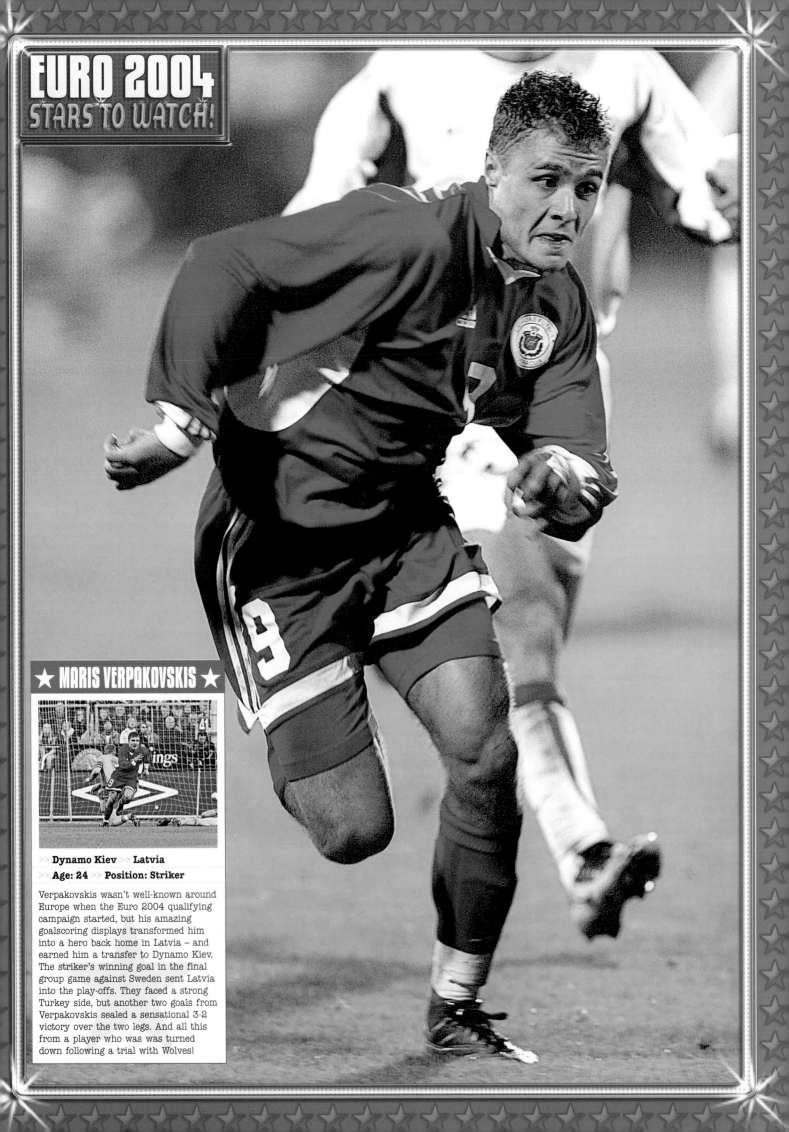

EURO 2004
STARS TO WATCH!

★ MARIS VERPAKOVSKIS ★

>> **Dynamo Kiev** >> **Latvia**
>> **Age: 24** >> **Position: Striker**

Verpakovskis wasn't well-known around Europe when the Euro 2004 qualifying campaign started, but his amazing goalscoring displays transformed him into a hero back home in Latvia – and earned him a transfer to Dynamo Kiev. The striker's winning goal in the final group game against Sweden sent Latvia into the play-offs. They faced a strong Turkey side, but another two goals from Verpakovskis sealed a sensational 3-2 victory over the two legs. And all this from a player who was was turned down following a trial with Wolves!

DA SECOND 'ARF OF ME EURO QUIZ IS 'ERE! GIVE IT A GO, THEN ADD UP YA SCORE FROM DA TWO 'ALVES TO SEE IF YOU IS A GENIUS!

HELP PERCY!

I'M STWUGGLING TO SPELL THESE NAMES PROPERLY! PWEASE HELP ME SPELL THEM COWWECTLY!

1. David Twezeggy — ANSWER
2. Wayne Wooney — ANSWER
3. Aliceandwo Nest — ANSWER
4. Cwistiano Wonaldo — ANSWER
5. Woaquin — ANSWER

2 POINTS FOR EACH CORRECT ANSWER — MY SCORE /10

MAMA-MIA MATCH-UP!

RECKON YA KNOW YER PIZZA FROM YER PASTA? SEE IF YA CAN MATCH THESE ITALY PLAYERS WIV THEIR SERIE A CLUBS!

1	CHRISTIAN VIERI	A	ROMA
2	FILIPPO INZAGHI	B	JUVENTUS
3	GIANLUIGI BUFFON	C	INTER MILAN
4	FRANCESCO TOTTI	D	LAZIO
5	STEFANO FIORE	E	AC MILAN

2 POINTS FOR EACH CORRECT ANSWER — MY SCORE /10

ORANGES!

CAN YA NAME DA FIVE DUTCH DUDES WOT ARE HIDIN' IN DA ORANGES?

ANSWER — ANSWER — ANSWER — ANSWER — ANSWER

2 POINTS FOR EACH CORRECT ANSWER — MY SCORE /10

EURO WORD SEARCH

THESE EURO STARS ARE ALL GOOD MATES O' MINE, BUT CAN YA SPOT 'EM ALL?

```
T W D A I Q I W U M J B F Y W W U E B J
I G D D C W T T Y U J R O O N E Y S Y A
U O X D G D N I R P V M J U G W U C H J
T P X J A M E S T L R E Y E S J F A B L
J N P F N E S E V A R G E L K O I M A U
C Q E I L O Q R Q E N A D I Z O K P L D
B T F V N E Y F F Y F U J S Y X K B L Q
I T N P I V Z C A N N A V A R O F E A E
W V I L S L X F D K E K O T R N I L C O
G A I J M N L P K U Z D L P L U G L K K
N R K K N D F E U R L Z G U W Z O S Q H
S I L V E S T R E A R E Z X I Q Z Z G A
X A C F A I J K N Z K U W Q V O G R M
Z B R E S K R O C O G C J K B L E G E A
V O F L R O R X M A K E L E L E S R L N
A Y M O A K R G O H N S G A C V S Y T N
W T T C H P R N Y H M Q G N P E V F H N
R A U L A J F I A T X V L I Y H I I B P
Y C P X P E S K Q N O S S N E V S R H N
```

> Ballack	> Gravesen	> Makelele	> Ronaldo
> Campbell	> Hamann	> Neville	> Rooney
> Cannavaro	> James	> Pahars	> Silvestre
> Cole	> Kahn	> Raul	> Svensson
> Figo	> Kluivert	> Reyes	> Zidane

1/2 POINT FOR EACH CORRECT ANSWER — MY SCORE /10

ENGLAND EXPECTS!

'OW MUCH DO YA KNOW ABOUT DA ENGLAND TEAM THEN? LET'S FIND OUT BY 'AVING A POP AT ME TEN QUESTIONS TO SEE 'OW MANY POINTS YA CAN GET!

1 England beat Slovakia in their first Euro 2004 qualifying match – but what was the final score? — ANSWER

2 Which of these three have won the most England caps – Emile Heskey, Frank Lampard or Ashley Cole? — ANSWER

3 England lost 3-2 in a friendly against Denmark last year, but at which Premiership ground was the game played? — ANSWER

4 Which Aston Villa ace scored the first goal in England's 2-0 win over Turkey in the Euro 2004 qualifiers? — ANSWER

5 And who scored the other goal from the penalty spot in the exciting game at the Stadium Of Light? — ANSWER

6 Which team knocked England out of the 2002 World Cup at the quarter-final stage? — ANSWER

7 England will take on Croatia, France and Switzerland in Group B, but which of these countries do they play first? — ANSWER

8 Which European rivals did England play in their last ever game at the old Wembley Stadium? — ANSWER

9 And who was the England gaffer then – was it Sven Goran Eriksson, Glenn Hoddle or Kevin Keegan? — ANSWER

10 Which Liverpool and England star is older – Steven Gerrard or Michael Owen? — ANSWER

1 POINT FOR EACH CORRECT ANSWER — MY SCORE /10

QUIZ!

WHO'S IN CHARGE?

CAN YA MATCH UP THESE GAFFERS WIV THE EURO TEAMS THEY MANAGE?

1 DICK ADVOCAAT	2 RUDI VOLLER	3 LUIZ FELIPE SCOLARI	4 GIOVANNI TRAPATTONI	5 JACQUES SANTINI

A ITALY	B FRANCE	C HOLLAND	D PORTUGAL	E GERMANY

2 POINTS FOR EACH CORRECT ANSWER

MY SCORE /10

HIDE & SEEK!

HAIRCUT

WHICH STRIKER IS HIDIN' UNDER THE MOP-TOP OF SPAIN STAR CARLOS PUYOL?

ANSWER

10 POINTS FOR CORRECT ANSWER

MY SCORE /10

ZINEDINE ZIDANE QUIZ!

WOT DO YA KNOW 'BOUT DA WORLD'S GREATEST FOOTY PLAYER? NOT AS MUCH AS ME, BUT 'AVE A GO!

1 Which Italian team did 'Zizou' used to play for between 1996 and 2001?

ANSWER

2 How much did Real Madrid pay for him?

ANSWER

3 Zidane scored the winner in the 2002 Champions League final – but who was it against?

ANSWER

4 What shirt number does Zizou wear for the mighty Real Madrid?

ANSWER

5 Who has won the most France caps – Zidane or Arsenal's Thierry Henry?

ANSWER

2 POINTS FOR EACH CORRECT ANSWER

MY SCORE /10

dream team!

TRY TO WORK OUT WHICH TOP EUROPEAN PLAYERS I'VE PICKED FOR ME DREAM TEAM. I'VE EVEN GIVEN YA DA 'KEEPER FOR FREE TO GET YA STARTED!

Germany & Bayern Munich No.1!

GK

Oliver Kahn

Spain & Real Madrid star! | **Holland's ex-Man. United defender!** | **Germany & Dortmund centre-back!** | **Italy's versatile Juventus star!**

RB — ANSWER | CB — ANSWER | CB — ANSWER | LB — ANSWER

Speedy Denmark & PSV winger! | **Portugal's experienced Milan man!** | **Roma star with the initials 'FT'!** | **Porto ace with a four-letter name!**

RM — ANSWER | CM — ANSWER | CM — ANSWER | LM — ANSWER

Sweden & Ajax striker! | **Switzerland & Basle trickster!**

 S — ANSWER | S — ANSWER

1 POINT FOR EACH CORRECT ANSWER

MY SCORE /10

SPOT THE DIFFERENCE!

THERE ARE FIVE DIFFERENCES BETWEEN THESE PICS, BUT CAN YA CIRCLE 'EM ALL?

2 POINTS FOR EACH CORRECT ANSWER

MY SCORE /10

ANSWERS

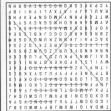

EURO 2004

61

62
Becks picks up an injury in training and could miss the quarter-finals!
Miss a turn

63

64

65
A last-minute Stevie G strike sees England beat Spain in the quarter-finals!
Take an extra turn

60
Rooney bags a hat-trick against Croatia as England win 4-1! You're through to the next stage!
Move to square 63

59

58
Despite creating loads of chances, England fail to score against Switzerland and draw 0-0.
Go back to square 44

57

56
Scholesy falls asleep by the hotel swimming pool and gets a nasty case of sunburn. Ou
Go back to square 36

41

42
With qualifying coming to a dramatic climax, things are tight at the top and your squad gets nervous!
Go back to square 21

43

44

45

40

39

38
You get linked with the Chelsea job and it unsettles your players!
Go back to square 25

37

36

21

22

23

24
Owen and Becks help you to a 2-0 win over Liechtenstein!
Take an extra turn

25

20
Your plan to try out new players goes wrong when you get whupped by Australia 3-1!
Miss a turn

19
You bring loads of quality youngsters into the squad for the first time!
Move to square 23

18

17
You only manage a 2-2 draw at home to Macedonia!
Miss a turn

16

START
Can you go all the way to the final and win Euro 2004?

2

3

4
You're drawn in a decent qualifying group with Slovakia, Turkey, Macedonia and Liechtenstein!
Move to square 16

5

GAME!

66
shley Cole's red card in the pain game means he'll be spended for the semi-final!
Go back to square 35

67
An Owen goal and a late header from Campbell seals a 2-1 win over Holland in the semis! Almost there!
Take an extra turn

68

69
It's Germany in the final! But your players reckon they're a bogey team!
Go back to square 51

FINISH
Becks scores a sudden-death penalty against Germany in the final! You've won it!

55

54
Amazing scenes as you start the tournament with a wicked 3-2 win over France!
Take an extra turn

53

52

51

46

47
A 0-0 draw against Turkey is just enough to qualify. You're on your way to Portugal!
Take an extra turn

48

49
You're drawn against France in the first game of Euro 2004. A defeat could really knock confidence!
Miss a turn

50

35

34
Wayne Rooney scores his first England goal in a win over Macedonia, then bags again against Liechtenstein!
Move to square 53

33

32

31

26

27
A wicked win against Turkey gets everyone in party mood!
Move to square 33

28

29

30
You can't decide which 'keeper should be your No.1. Should it be Jamo, Robbo or someone else?
Miss a turn

15

14

13

12
A few Premiership gaffers complain about you nabbing their star players!
Miss a turn

11
Michael Owen bags a late goal in a 2-1 win over Slovakia!
Move to square 29

6

7

8
Your players think they'll qualify easily, so they ease up a bit in training!
Go back to square 6

9

Using your weekly copy of **MATCH**, fill in the results of each game, then write the names of the teams as they qualify for each stage – right up to the Euro 2004 final on July 4 in Lisbon!

GROUP A PORTUGAL > GREECE > SPAIN > RUSSIA

PORTUGAL v GREECE	RUSSIA v PORTUGAL
June 12, 5.00pm in Porto	June 16, 7.45pm in Lisbon

SPAIN v RUSSIA	SPAIN v PORTUGAL
June 12, 7.45pm in Faro-Loule	June 20, 7.45pm in Lisbon

GREECE v SPAIN	RUSSIA v GREECE
June 16, 5.00pm in Porto	June 20, 7.45pm in Faro-Loule

GROUP B ENGLAND > FRANCE > SWITZERLAND > CROATIA

SWITZERLAND v CROATIA	CROATIA v FRANCE
June 13, 5.00pm in Leiria	June 17, 7.45pm in Leiria

FRANCE v ENGLAND	SWITZERLAND v FRANCE
June 13, 7.45pm in Lisbon	June 21, 7.45pm in Coimbra

ENGLAND v SWITZERLAND	CROATIA v ENGLAND
June 17, 5.00pm in Coimbra	June 21, 7.45pm in Lisbon

GROUP C ITALY > SWEDEN > DENMARK > BULGARIA

DENMARK v ITALY	ITALY v SWEDEN
June 14, 5.00pm in Guimaraes	June 18, 7.45pm in Porto

SWEDEN v BULGARIA	ITALY v BULGARIA
June 14, 7.45pm in Lisbon	June 22, 7.45pm in Guimaraes

BULGARIA v DENMARK	DENMARK v SWEDEN
June 18, 5.00pm in Braga	June 22, 7.45pm in Porto

GROUP D CZECH REPUBLIC > GERMANY > HOLLAND > LATVIA

CZECH REP. v LATVIA	HOLLAND v CZECH REP.
June 15, 5.00pm in Aveiro	June 19, 7.45pm in Aveiro

GERMANY v HOLLAND	HOLLAND v LATVIA
June 15, 7.45pm in Porto	June 23, 7.45pm in Braga

LATVIA v GERMANY	GERMANY v CZECH REP.
June 19, 5.00pm in Porto	June 23, 7.45pm in Lisbon

QUARTER-FINAL ONE — June 24, 7.45pm in Lisbon

GROUP A WINNERS
GROUP B RUNNERS-UP

QUARTER-FINAL TWO — June 25, 7.45pm in Lisbon

GROUP B WINNERS
GROUP A RUNNERS-UP

QUARTER-FINAL THREE — June 26, 7.45pm in Faro-Loule

GROUP C WINNERS
GROUP D RUNNERS-UP

QUARTER-FINAL FOUR — June 27, 7.45pm in Porto

GROUP D WINNERS
GROUP C RUNNERS-UP

FIXTURES GUIDE!

SEMI-FINAL ONE	June 30, 7.45pm in Lisbon
QUARTER-FINAL ONE WINNERS	
QUARTER-FINAL THREE WINNERS	

THE EURO 2004 FINAL!	July 4, 7.45pm in Lisbon
SEMI-FINAL ONE WINNERS	
SEMI-FINAL TWO WINNERS	

SEMI-FINAL TWO	July 1, 7.45pm in Porto
QUARTER-FINAL TWO WINNERS	
QUARTER-FINAL FOUR WINNERS	

FINAL WHISTLE!

SEE YA LATER!

GIVE THE MATCH READERS A BIG HAND, LADS!

SEE YA AT THE WORLD CUP 2006, FOR SURE!

MATCH! EURO 2004 CHECKLIST!

Tick off these boxes during Euro 2004 and try to get the lot!

I sang the national anthem in my living room before England games!
✗ ✔

I saw Cristiano Ronaldo do a double stepover then fall on his backside!
✗ ✔

I told mum I was ill so that I could stay at home to watch the footy! Ssshhh!
✗ ✔

I ran around my back garden screaming like a loony when England scored!
✗ ✔

I saw Henry bamboozle two defenders and hammer in a wonder goal!
✗ ✔

I went absolutely bananas when England beat France in their first game!
✗ ✔

I wore my England shirt every single day for the whole competition!
✗ ✔

I watched so many matches I went footy mad and slept with my boots on!
✗ ✔

I saw David Beckham bend in a brilliant free-kick from 30 yards out!
✗ ✔

I read every single page of my MATCH Euro 2004 Guide – twice!
✗ ✔

1 Wonderkid Wayne Rooney was still lurking in the Everton reserve team in June 2002, but now he's a footy megastar and ready to bang in the goals for England!

2 All the matches will be on TV at normal times, so unlike the 2002 World Cup, you won't have to crawl out of bed at stupid times in the morning to watch them! What a bonus!

10 REASONS WHY...

EURO 2004 WILL BE BETTER THAN WORLD CUP 2002!

3 Brazil won't be playing at Euro 2004 because the country is not in Europe – so that means Ronaldinho can't lob our 'keeper and knock us out of the tournament like he did at the last World Cup!

4 England midfield ace Steven Gerrard was injured for the 2002 World Cup, but he'll be mixing it up in Portugal this summer! And England have never lost a competitive game with him in the side! Get in!

5 The tournament is being hosted by footy-crazy Portugal – home of some well-flash new footy stadiums and ultra-skilful stars like Luis Figo, Cristiano Ronaldo and Rui Costa! It should be wicked!

6 England captain David Beckham was brilliant in the 2002 World Cup – but now he's a Real Madrid hero, which means we've got a player who can mix it with France's Zinedine Zidane and Spain's Raul!

7 Holland didn't make it to the last World Cup finals, but they'll be at Euro 2004 with a squad of stars like Davids, Kluivert and Van Nistelrooy! And don't forget their army of mad, orange-faced fans!

8 The only European teams to get further than England in World Cup 2002 were Turkey and Germany. Turkey haven't qualified for Euro 2004 and Sven's boys know they can easily stuff Germany 5-1 again!

9 Portugal is way nearer to England than South Korea and Japan, so there will be loads of Sven's barmy army flying to Portugal, ready to cheer the England boys on every step of the way to the final!

10 England lost out to Brazil in the World Cup quarter-finals in 2002, but with stars like Wayne Rooney, Franky Lamps and Stevie G now in the team, they can go all the way and become European Champs in 2004!

THEY THINK IT'S ALL OVER - BUT IT AIN'T!

Phweeep! The 90 minutes are up and you've reached the end of MATCH's Euro 2004 Guide! But don't forget you can keep up-to-date with all the latest Euro 2004 news, exclusive interviews and footy gossip during the tournament by bagging your copy of MATCH every Tuesday! And look out for some wicked free Euro 2004 gifts as well! See ya soon, footy dudes!